MOMENTUM CULTURE

HOW HIGH-PERFORMING COMPANIES LEVERAGE
CULTURE FOR COMPETITIVE ADVANTAGE

BY MATT PROSTKO

Printed in the United States of America

First Printing, 2024

ISBN 978-0-9996441-4-0

Written by Matt Prostko
www.momentumculture.com

TABLE OF CONTENTS

Preface

I. Introduction

II. The Momentum Culture Framework

III. The MOMENTuM Process

IV. Call to Action

References

PREFACE

I am fascinated by organizational culture.

In my years of working across various industries, I've encountered a wide range of them. Some were extraordinary—energizing environments where you could feel the collective drive and passion in the air. Others, not so much. Some were actually caustic to the people that worked there. The difference between being part of a great culture and a mediocre one is profound. It can make the difference between winning and losing as a business, and it can significantly shape people's careers and even their worldview on life and work, for the rest of their lives.

After spending my career in different companies, I've seen firsthand the impact culture has on business outcomes. But it wasn't until I conducted interviews to explore the notion of culture that I grasped how deeply it touches people. That's when I knew I had to do something to help organizations create and sustain amazing cultures—ones where employees can feel that same positive energy and drive that leads to success.

Our world is changing rapidly. The shift to more hybrid and remote work, along with the relentless pace of globalization and technological advancements, has altered how employees connect with each other and their organizations. These changes make it even more critical to understand and cultivate a strong organizational culture—one that can serve as a unique competitive advantage in an increasingly fast-paced environment.

This book introduces the Momentum Culture Framework—a data-driven approach that explains how cultural energy within an organization is created, directed, and accelerated toward achieving company goals. The framework offers practical, actionable insights that can help you target the elements of your culture that are most strongly correlated with business success.

Whether you're planning a full-scale cultural transformation or just looking for ways to strengthen your existing culture, this book provides a blueprint for success. By following the framework and process outlined in these pages, you'll be able to create a cultural flywheel—one that generates business momentum, driving better results more consistently, with less effort, and less investment over time.

If you believe that culture can be a driving force in your business and in your people's lives, this book is written for you. It's my hope that the insights and tools I share here will help you cultivate the kind of culture where people love to work, and where business thrives as a result.

Welcome to the journey of building a Momentum Culture. Let's get started.

SECTION

1

INTRODUCTION

WHY CULTURE?

Why is it that culture is often described as the ultimate competitive advantage, yet so many culture change efforts fail so spectacularly? Peter Drucker said it best: "Culture eats strategy for breakfast." But if 70% of culture change initiatives fall flat[1], it's turning out to be a pretty expensive breakfast. Leaders know culture is crucial, but the path to their desired organizational culture is often clouded in vagueness and uncertainty.

This book introduces a culture framework that provides the clarity and direction leaders need. This isn't just another set of fluffy ideals or vague suggestions. This is a statistically proven, yet simple, blueprint for transforming culture from an aspirational idea into a strategic asset that drives consistent, measurable business results.

The challenge with traditional approaches to culture is that they often lack the clarity needed for real change. Leaders are frequently overwhelmed with well-intentioned advice that doesn't provide practical solutions. While traditional engagement surveys can highlight dissatisfaction among employees, they fall short of explaining the underlying reasons or offering concrete steps to improve. What leaders truly need are actionable insights and a clear, strategic path to foster a thriving organizational culture.

One of the key issues with traditional views on organizational culture is that the concept has been incomplete. This framework changes the game by recognizing that culture isn't just about employee feelings and behaviors. It's about integrating these human elements with the orga-

---

[1] (Kotter, Sense of Urgency, 2008)

nization's structures, processes, and capabilities. Think of it as creating a cultural flywheel—when connection (relationships) and capability (processes) align, they generate and store energy, providing the consistent horsepower you need to drive your organization forward. That is why we call it the Momentum Culture Framework.

Extensive research has shown that companies with strong cultures deliver up to four times better business results[2]. But achieving this requires more than good intentions. It requires a data-driven approach that integrates connection and capability to create a self-sustaining flywheel effect. The Momentum Culture Framework provides a comprehensive assessment tool and a recommendation engine, offering targeted insights that ensure your investments in cultural change are both effective and efficient. We have gathered a tremendous amount of data through this assessment tool, and this book unpacks the insights from that data in a simple, no-nonsense way. These data and insights can help you focus your investments, so that your culture can drive better business results. with more consistency and less resources, over time.

Are you tired of paying more each year for a breakfast that never satisfies? This book is here to give you the clarity and direction needed to transform your culture into a dynamic force for business success. Get data-driven advice on how to drive cultural improvement with more consistency (a more satisfying breakfast) that consumes less resources over time. Dive in and discover how to harness the power of culture and turn it into your competitive advantage. If you have been frustrated by throwing money at the issue year after year with no ROI, this book was written for you.

If you're serious about transforming your culture into the competitive edge that drives your business forward, this is your blueprint for success. Invest one day in reading and reflecting on the insights within, and you'll unlock the keys to a culture that delivers measurable results,

---

[2] (Kotter, Corporate Culture and Performance, 2011)

consistently and efficiently. This can help you deliver the critical shift your organization needs. Don't let another year of wasted resources pass you by—dive in, and let's start building a culture that works as hard as you do.

CULTURE AS COMPETTIVE ADVANTAGE

The Pursuit of Culture for Sustainable Competitive Advantage

The pursuit of organizational culture as a means to gain a competitive edge is not new. It dates back to the 1950s, when Dr. Elliot Jaques first introduced the concept in his book The Changing Culture of a Factory. However, it wasn't until the early 1980s that the concept of culture truly entered the mainstream. Seminal works like Corporate Cultures: The Rites and Rituals of Corporate Life by Terrence Deal and Allan Kennedy, and In Search of Excellence by Tom Peters and Robert Waterman, popularized the idea that culture could be a powerful driver of business success. These books sparked a wave of interest, leading many organizations to invest heavily in cultural initiatives during the 1980s and 1990s, as they sought to adapt to competitive pressures, technological changes, and globalization.

In a business landscape where market advantages come and go with the speed of technological change, the quest for something enduring—something that can consistently drive performance—has never been more critical. In this environment, companies are under immense pressure to cultivate a culture that adapts and thrives amidst constant change. As we discussed in the introduction, culture is increasingly recognized as an enduring force, with the potential to deliver sustained competitive advantage.

But what do we really mean by organizational culture? Edgar Schein, a leading expert on organizational culture, defines it as the set of shared assumptions a group learns as it solves problems of external adaptation and internal integration. These assumptions form the foundation of an organization's values, behaviors, and norms.

Through the research that underpins this book, I have arrived at a slightly more expansive definition. The data indicates that culture is defined by more than shared beliefs and behavior norms. It is the intersection of organizational capabilities and human connections – how organizational structures and processes influence human behavior, and how employees connect with fellow co-workers, customers and the organization itself. This book is about uncovering those principles and helping you build a strong organizational culture that drives business results.

Uncovering the Real Need

Over the past few years, I've had the privilege of speaking about organizational culture with dozens of CEOs and CHROs from a diverse range of industries. A common theme emerged in these conversations: a deep-seated frustration with the inefficiency of current cultural efforts. These leaders were all searching for the same thing—a "culture" that could deliver measurable, sustainable results. As I probed deeper, asking what they really meant by "culture", it became clear that what they were truly seeking was an approach to investing in their people and processes in a way that would generate an ROI, and that would demonstrate leverage over time. What these leaders truly want is to see their investments begin to stack, to build upon each other, and to deliver either the same level of performance for less investment over time or the same level of investment with asymmetrically positive returns.

The Momentum Culture Framework

This is the ultimate goal of any corporation—turning linear investments into geometric returns. To that end, academically, strategy is often referred to as a "Model for Above Average Returns". Or in simpler terms, an effective strategy is an approach to creating an above-market return on the assets of the firm. Similarly, a great culture is a way of working that enables, supports, or even drives above average returns. The Momentum Culture Framework was developed to provide leaders with a clear, evidence-based approach to building a culture that not only drives performance but does so in a sustainable, self-reinforcing way.

What is a Great Culture?

Since the prevailing research proves that culture is highly correlated to business performance, then a weak culture leads to operations that sputter, wobble, and jerk— characterized by inconsistency and unpredictability. In contrast, a strong culture, whether it's positive or negative, smooths performance and creates consistency through momentum. Research by Sorenson[3] has shown that firms with strong cultures experience less volatile cash flows, suggesting reduced performance variability. A Momentum Culture ensures consistent delivery of desired goals with high leverage—better results over time with more consistency, and less investment. It is a culture that not only drives performance but does so in a way that amplifies the impact and efficiency of every investment made.

Conclusion

In essence, the core concepts and beliefs behind the Momentum Culture Framework revolve around the idea of creating a strong culture that delivers sustained, leveraged performance. In adapting the framework to their organization, leaders can begin to build an environment that not only supports their strategic goals but also drives them forward with increasing efficiency and effectiveness. As we move forward, we'll delve into the research methods that underpin this framework, providing the empirical foundation that makes these concepts actionable and reliable.

---

[3] (Sorenson, 2001)

THE RESEARCH

A Data-Driven Quest for Cultural Excellence

To truly crack the code of what makes some organizations consistently outperform their peers, we need a rigorous, data-driven approach. The Momentum Culture Framework is built on a strong foundation of empirical evidence, derived from a systematic research process designed to uncover the factors that set high-performing cultures apart.

The goal of our research was clear: to clarify the unique characteristics of cultures in companies that consistently outperform their peers. This section outlines the research process that led to the discovery of these key drivers, providing the empirical backbone for the Momentum Culture Framework.

Defining the Research Goal

To do this, the first step was to create a comprehensive list—a superset— of possible cultural characteristics to test. This would serve as the foundation for identifying the factors that truly drive success. To build this superset of characteristics, we began with a broad review of the most relevant research and publications on corporate culture. These sources were coupled with dozens of interviews with a wide range of CEOs and CHROs. These leaders provided practical insights and shared their experiences with cultural initiatives, offering a real-world perspective on what they believed comprised a successful culture. Combining these two sources—the theoretical and the practical—we were able to create a set of 10 possible factors that seemed most likely to be the drivers of successful cultures.

Selecting the Sample: High vs. Low Performing Companies

With our list of possible cultural characteristics in hand, the next step was to identify the companies that would serve as our study subjects. We focused on the S&P 500, breaking these companies into industry groups to ensure a fair comparison. Any companies that didn't fit into clear industry classifications or lacked obvious peer companies were eliminated from the study to maintain the integrity of our comparisons.

We then conducted a retrospective analysis of shareholder value creation over a decade, a period that included both boom and bust cycles. This long-term view allowed us to identify companies that performed consistently well or poorly relative to their peers. Companies that were a standard deviation better or worse than the mean were classified as high or low performers, respectively. Neutral performers were eliminated from the study to ensure a clear distinction between the two groups.

Data Collection: Survey Design and Execution

To gather meaningful data, we needed to create a survey that could generate deep insights into the specific drivers of each cultural factor. We developed 10 questions for each of the 10 topic areas, ensuring that the questions were designed to elicit specific, actionable responses.

This survey was conducted among employees at both the high and low performing companies identified in our sample selection process. By collecting data from over 100 companies, we ensured that our data set was both broad and deep, providing a rich source of information for analysis.

Analysis: Identifying Performance Predictors

Our goal was to determine how the responses from high-performing companies differed from those of low performers. We conducted regression analysis to identify the factors that predicted higher performance.

Through this rigorous analysis, we were able to isolate the factors that truly mattered. Six factors rose to the top, each with specific elements that consistently predicted high performance. These factors would become the cornerstone of the Momentum Culture Model.

Wave 2: Refining and Expanding the Research

Building on the success of our initial research, we embarked on a second wave of data collection and analysis. We refined our assessment tool, narrowing down the factors and questions to focus on what truly mattered. The new tool included 50 total questions, with a mix of overarching questions and specific questions for each of the six key factors.

This refined survey was delivered to a larger group of companies, resulting in data from hundreds of organizations and over 1,000 responses. The company data is organized across industries and company sizes. There were subtle differences in Momentum in these slices, but the variance was not statistically significant.

The individual responses are categorized by functional role, role level, and region, and there were meaningful differences in these areas. With respect to function, human resources professionals tended to perceive a higher level of momentum than did people in the manufacturing function. Respondents in Asia had a lower perception of culture than did either Europe/Middle East (EMEA) or the Americas. And predictably, Senior Executives tended to assess the culture of their organizations more positively than either managers or individual contributors. They key here was to analyze the amount of drop off from level to level – some is expected, too much predicts a low trust culture.

The analysis of the complete data set yielded some surprising insights and led to the development of a simple yet powerful framework for interpreting corporate culture. This framework now serves as the foundation for Momentum Culture, offering leaders a clear, actionable path to building a culture that drives sustained high performance.

Conclusion

The research process that defined the Momentum Culture Framework was methodical, rigorous, and data driven. By identifying and validating the key factors that drive cultural success, we've laid the foundation for a framework that leaders can trust to deliver results. In the next chapter, we'll explore the insights derived from this research, setting the stage for the practical application of the Momentum Culture Framework. These insights will help you not only understand what makes a culture thrive but also how to implement these lessons in your own organization.

THE FLYWHEEL

The Flywheel of Connection and Capability

After establishing a data-driven foundation for understanding culture, the research pointed to something profound. It became clear that the key to a thriving culture wasn't just in identifying various factors in isolation—it was about recognizing the critical balance of connection and capability. This integration creates a cultural flywheel, a self-sustaining energy source that propels organizations toward success when both elements are in harmony.

The Power of Capability

For the purposes of this discussion, Capability is defined by structures and processes that enable core organizational competencies through people. One of the more profound insights that came from the research was the strong correlation of a few key organizational capabilities to the perception of effective culture. Moreover, this correlation exists to a higher degree than more commonplace notions of the source of culture. It makes perfect sense though. When a company has strong fundamental capabilities, it operates smoothly, delivering consistent results that fuel the cultural flywheel. Success breeds confidence in employees, and confidence strengthens the culture, creating a positive feedback loop that drives further success.

However, when there are weaknesses in critical capabilities, the impact is similarly profound. Ineffectiveness creates an atmosphere of doubt or failure that saps the organization's energy. This lack of capability not only disrupts operations but also affects how employees perceive the company from within. Humans naturally resist seeing themselves as failures, so when the company they work for is failing, they begin to disassociate, distancing themselves from the organization. This disassociation breaks the connection employees feel with the company and its culture, causing the flywheel to stall.

The "We-They" Characterization

A telling sign in the research data is the shift in language from "We" to "They." When we examined comments from respondents who doubted the organization's competence, they tended to refer to the company in the third person. This subtle but significant change in language indicates a deeper disconnect—a shift from feeling part of the organization to viewing it as something separate. John F. Kennedy famously commented after the Bay of Pigs fiasco that "Success has many fathers, but failure is an orphan", and our research indicates that this dynamic plays out in corporate culture as well. The research data reinforced a simple but powerful truth: Capability is king. Confidence in the organization's ability to execute feeds success, and success feeds the culture.

The Role of Connection

The research illuminated the notion of Connection, the depth and the ways in which employees of a company relate to each other, to their customers, to management, and to the organization itself. While capability is crucial, it's connection that forms the foundation for full effort and engagement from employees. According to the book 9 Lies About Work, one of the most pervasive misconceptions is that people care which company they work for. In reality, people care more about the team they're on, because that's where the real work happens. People may join an organization whose purpose jives with their own, but they give their full effort to support the people on either side of them – not the company logo. This insight was supported by this research and underscores the importance of connection among employees in creating a high-performance culture.

Our interviews with leaders from high-performing organizations consistently highlighted the role of connection. In these companies, there was a palpable sense of camaraderie and even fun among employees. Time was deliberately made to bring people together in meaningful ways, fostering friendships that would carry teams through tough times or crunch periods. In these environments, the grind was seen not as a punishment, but as a bonding experience—an opportunity to strengthen relationships and deepen connection.

> *"Work and play are words used to describe the same thing under differing conditions."*

—Mark Twain

This sentiment was reflected in the cultures of the organizations we studied. Many of the situations were the same, but the perceptions could be vastly different. In cultures where connection was strong, work felt less like a burden and more like a shared journey. This difference in perception is a testament to the power of culture in shaping how employees experience their work.

The Relationship Between Capability and Connection

The data analysis validated the inclusion of the Factors of Momentum that define Capability and Connection. Statistically, they both strongly predict the independent measurement of Momentum, with Capability doing so more significantly. The chart below shows their relative impact.

Magnitude of Prediction of Momentum

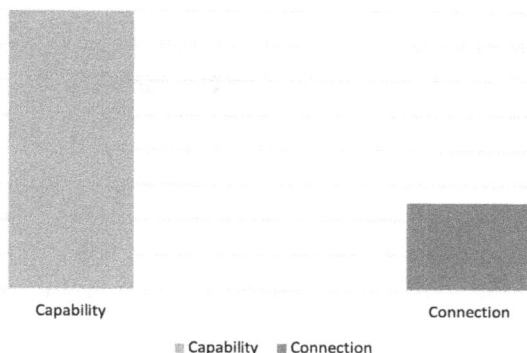

Capability		Connection

■ Capability ■ Connection

While Capability and Connection, as we define them, work together to create Momentum, they are unique from one another. They demonstrated discriminant validity – meaning that while they both strongly predicted Momentum, they did not statistically predict each other. This proves that they are truly unique constructions that are measuring different things, so both are needed to create an accurate picture of organizational culture.

Conclusion

At the core of the Momentum Culture Framework lies the intersection of connection and capability. These two elements are intertwined, each fueling the other in a self-sustaining cycle, keeping the cultural flywheel in motion. As we move forward, the next chapter will explore the Momentum Culture Framework itself, providing a practical guide for leaders to implement these insights in their own organizations. This framework offers a clear path to building a culture that not only survives but thrives in today's competitive landscape.

MOMENTUM CULTURE DESIGN AND MEASUREMENT

Framework Design

In our exploration of the essential balance between connection and capability, we've uncovered the elements that drive cultural success. The Momentum Culture Framework is designed to make sense of these elements by providing a structure that makes it easier to understand, and a set of metrics that allow you to objectively measure your current culture. In this chapter we will lay out those structures and measurements.

Fusion, Vector, and Velocity: The Properties of a Momentum Culture

As we have discussed, organizational culture is shaped by the intersection of Capability and Connection. The Momentum Culture Model is defined by three such intersections we refer to as Properties: Fusion, Vector, and Velocity, each describing a different aspect of how connection and capability interact within the organization. Each of these intersections of Capability and Connection create two new Dynamics that create momentum in the culture.

Fusion is about creating energy by bringing people and ideas together. It enables collaboration and innovation, reflecting the organization's ability to connect individuals in ways that drive both personal and organizational growth. Fusion is defined by the combination of the Capability of Learning & Innovation and the Trust & Collaboration that defines the Connection between coworkers. Each of these factors drive the momentum of the culture, but their intersection creates two key Dynamics which further describe it; Psychological Safety, the confidence to be able to challenge the status quo, and Coherence, the synchrony of words and actions from management.

Vector provides direction to the energy created in Fusion, ensuring that the efforts of employees align with the organization's strategic goals and value creation. It is shaped by the relationship between employees and the external market, particularly their connection to customers. Vector is comprised of the organization's Capability to Align to Vision and Strategy and the employees' Connection to customers within its Customer Orientation. The combination of these two Factors defines two key cultural Dynamics, Coordinating Incentives, rewarding employees for creating real market value, and Driving Execution, the ability to deliver desired outcomes on time.

Velocity accelerates organizational performance by empowering employees to make decisions and holding them accountable for the outcomes. It is defined by the relationship between employees and their managers, with an emphasis on autonomy and accountability. Velocity is the integration the Connection created by Empowerment and Accountability – the balance of freedom and responsibility, and the Capability of the organization around Decision Making. These two factors combine to create two new Dynamics; Encouraging Growth, incentivizing activities that feed business results, and Providing Clarity, reducing complexity for workers.

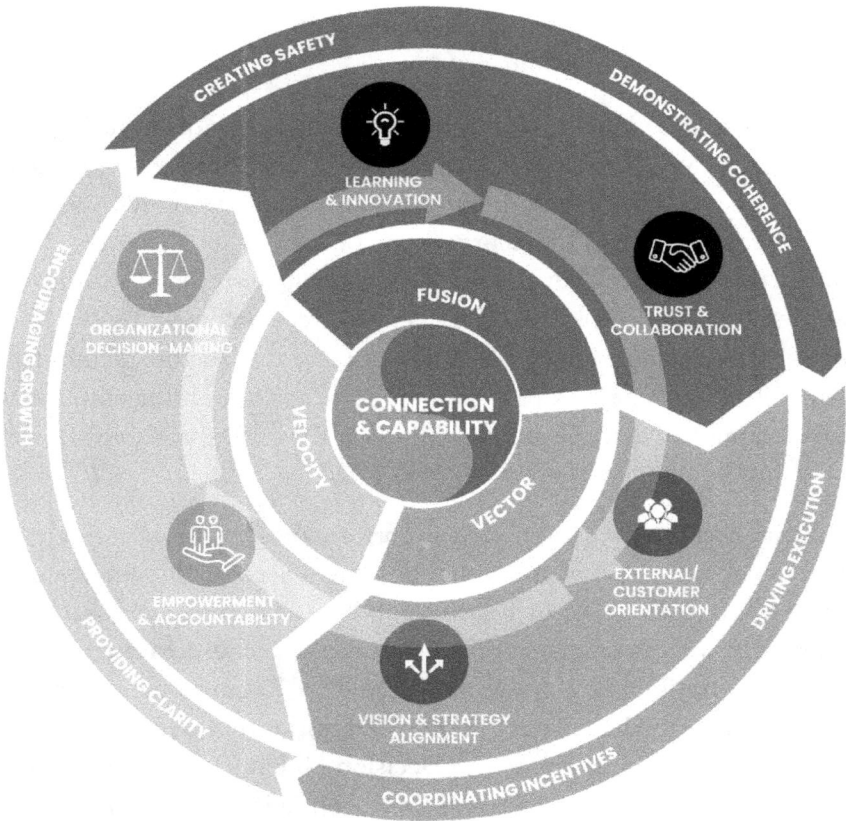

These Properties of Fusion, Vector and Velocity work together as a self-reinforcing cycle to create a Momentum Culture that actively drives the organization's strategic objectives.

Defining the Momentum Culture Model

Culture is more than just the collective mindsets and behaviors of the employees within an organization. It is shaped by both intrinsic and extrinsic factors from both the employees and the organization itself. Culture is not separate from the organization's strategy, structure, and processes, it is deeply embedded within them, influencing and being influenced by how employees interact with them. Those interactions create perceptions – in how employees perceive the organization, and concurrently, how the organization regards the employees. A Momentum Culture is defined by the dynamic interaction between these factors, where both intrinsic elements—like values and mindsets—and extrinsic elements—like behaviors and organizational capabilities—work in harmony. That balance is what drives sustained performance, making culture a powerful engine rather than just a backdrop.

MOMENTUM CULTURE MODEL

	Organization	Employees
Intrinsic	*Values:* The core principles and ethical standards that guide decision-making and behavior within the organization. Structures & Resources: The formal organizational design, physical assets, and tools available that support and shape the functioning of the organization.	*Mindsets:* The underlying beliefs and attitudes that influence how individuals perceive the world and approach their work. Skills: The abilities and expertise that individuals possess, which enable them to perform specific tasks effectively.
Extrinsic	*Processes & Capabilities:* The systematic methods and competencies that enable the organization to achieve its strategic goals and perform its activities.	*Behaviors:* The observable actions and conduct of individuals, shaped by their mindsets and skills, within the organizational context.
Perceptions	*How the organization regards employees:* The organization's view of its workforce, encompassing the recognition, appreciation, and support of employees' contributions and well-being.	*How employees regard the organization:* The collective feelings and judgments that employees hold about their organization's culture, values, and practices.

The Momentum Culture Model is grounded in a clear understanding of how intrinsic and extrinsic factors interact within both individuals and organizations. For individuals, Mindsets drive what they will do, while Skills determine what they can do. For organizations, Values define what they support and admonish, while Structures and Resources indicate what they will invest in. For individuals, Behaviors are the outward manifestation of their Mindsets and Skills. In organizations, capabilities, rules, and processes reflect the organization's values, structures, and resources, delineating what the organization enables and requires employees to do. These interactions shape both how employees perceive the organization and how management perceives the employees. These perceptions are the underpinnings of culture. The Momentum Culture Framework uses this Model to more comprehensively describe each Factor, and each chapter includes a tailored version of this table. That detail forms the basis of reflective questions and tactical suggestions on how you can reshape your organizational culture to build Momentum.

Measuring Momentum

But to begin growing your culture, you need a quantifiable measure to know where you are starting from. The Momentum Culture Assessment offers a robust set of data and analysis to give you a detailed baseline of measurement. There are three core metrics and tools that give you a clear understanding of where your culture sits today.

The Momentum Score

The Momentum Score provides a quantitative measure of the overall cultural energy within the organization. It's calculated using a metaphor for Einstein's formula for energy - $E=mc^2$. In this framework, "m" represents the core level of employee cultural "buy-in", and "c" represents both the level of Connection employees perceive, and their level of belief in the organization's Capabilities. This score provides a quantified baseline, assesses the health of their culture, and identifies areas for improvement within the organization.

For ease of interpretation, the Momentum Score is normalized to 100. So, if you had a perfect average score of 5.0 in every element of the formula, you would have a Momentum Score of 100 – a very unlikely outcome. So, while the internal score variance is the most insightful comparison, a Momentum Score that is over 50 represents a strong cultural perception, while scores below 25 are concerning. Given this structure and the large sample size of different companies and cultures, as you might imagine, the average Momentum Score is roughly 50.

Cultural Energy Efficiency

To provide a deeper breakdown, the Assessment unpacks the overall energy within the culture, acknowledging that there are positive and negative forces within every organization. These forces are determined by the breakdown of employee perception of the culture and the resulting impact on the organization's cultural energy.

Kinetic Energy is the percentage of energy in the organization that is positive and being actively directed towards driving toward the desired goals.

Potential Energy is the percentage of energy in an organization that is neutral and represents both an opportunity and a threat to the success of the culture.

Negative Energy is the percentage of energy in the organization that is negative and being actively directed against the company culture.

ENERGY EFFICIENCY

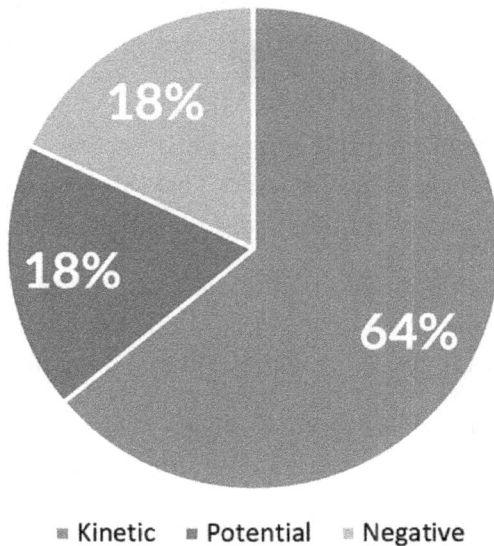

18%

18%

64%

■ Kinetic   ■ Potential   ■ Negative

For the overall dataset, respondents were predominantly Kinetic, more than a third of the organization was either not tangibly contributing to cultural energy or were actively sabotaging it. By analyzing this breakdown for their companies, leaders can understand how effectively the available cultural energy is being recruited to drive business results, and how much is being wasted.

The Momentum Matrix: Understanding Cultural Perceptions

The Momentum Score and the Cultural Energy Efficiency are measurements for the organization as a whole. But the organization is made up of individuals that all perceive the culture in their own unique way. To help make sense of these individual perspectives, we created the Momentum Matrix. a tool for assessing how employees regard the culture based on their perception of connection and capability. The Matrix categorizes those perceptions and interprets how those categories interact with the organization and their coworkers. The matrix categorizes employees into several groups:

Flywheels are deeply connected and perceive the organization as highly capable, contributing significantly to positive cultural energy and driving the business forward.

Collaborators maintain strong connections but may have some doubts about the organization's capabilities. They are generally happy but might question the organization's future success.

Executors are highly capable but may feel disconnected from their coworkers. They are certain of their skills and the fundamentals of the business but don't fully engage with the broader organizational culture.

Club Members are well-integrated with other stakeholders but lack belief in the organization's strategy, often dampening confidence in others.

Mercenaries are effective in their roles but lack connection to their coworkers or management, focusing more on personal advancement than organizational success.

Saboteurs actively undermine the culture, holding cynical views of the company's prospects and fostering negativity within the organization.

CULTURE PERSONAS MATRIX

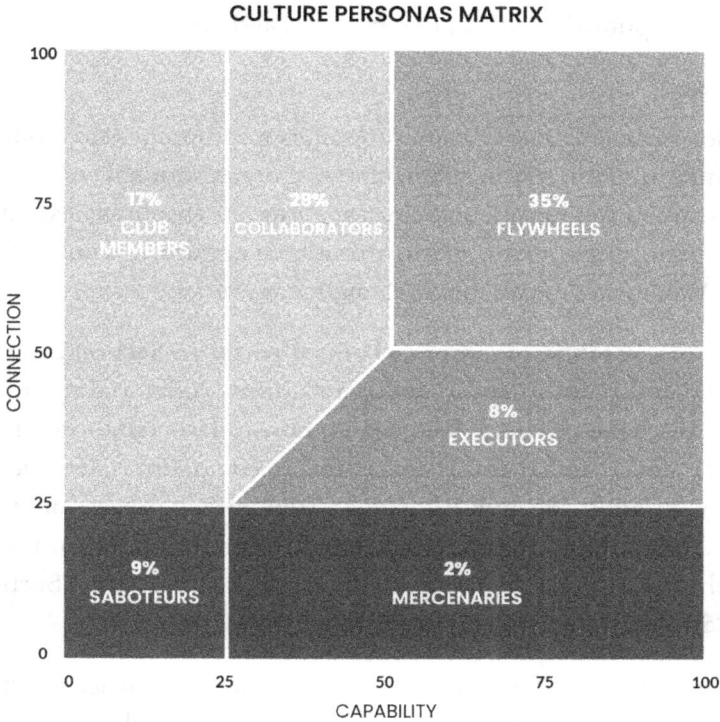

This framework highlights two of the key insights from the research. Firstly, that employee perception of key organizational Capabilities is a more reliable predictor of the perception of company culture than that of Connection to stakeholders. And secondly, that the confidence in Capability is also comparatively weaker than that of Connection. As a result, the research asserts that investment in cultural bonding activities that do not improve perception in core organizational competencies are likely going to be less effective.

But the matrix also provides insight into how perceptions are distributed throughout the organization and how they can be clustered into personas that characterize their perspective of company culture. Each of these personas interact with and contribute to the culture differently, and the organization's people strategy must be tailored to address these variations, optimizing cultural momentum and minimizing friction.

Conclusion

The Momentum Culture Framework offers a comprehensive approach to defining, quantifying and characterizing organizational culture. And while a strong framework and clear analysis are absolutely essential if you are going to improve your organizational culture, it is only half the battle. What you do with that information is every bit as important.

This book is essentially comprised of two parts. In Section II, we will take a deep dive into the Momentum Culture Model and the unique insights from the research, focusing on how to leverage those insights to create a culture that drives a sustainable competitive advantage for your organization. Section III details a step-by-step process on how to utilize those cultural insights to create the organizational culture that will deliver a sustainable momentum to your business. So, if Section II is the "So What", then Section III is the "Now What".

So, with that understanding, let's explore what we learned in the research about organizational culture, how those insights shaped the Momentum Culture Framework, what you can do with those insights to make your company culture a competitive advantage that can't be stopped or replicated.

THE MOMENTUM CULTURE FRAMEWORK

FUSION

Nuclear fusion - nu·cle·ar fu·sion - /ˌno͞oklēər ˈfyo͞oZH(ə)n/

a nuclear reaction in which atomic nuclei of low atomic number fuse to form a heavier nucleus with the release of energy.

Cultural fusion - cul·tur·al fu·sion - /ˈkəlCH(ə)rəl ˈfyo͞oZH(ə)n/

An organizational reaction in which individuals collaboratively engage in learning and problem solving, creating a connected organization with new ideas and new energy.

6

FUSION

Harnessing Collective Energy – Fusion's Role in Transforming Challenges into Opportunities

What if your organization's greatest strength was its ability to turn challenges into opportunities? In a business landscape that is increasingly defined by its complexities and uncertainties, the true test of an organization's culture lies in its capacity to continuously learn, adapt, innovate, and thrive in environments of constant change. This chapter explores the concept of Fusion within the Momentum Culture framework- the process of bringing people and ideas together, generating new energy that propels the organization forward. It's where the synergistic elements of your culture—trust, collaboration, learning, and innovation—come together to create something greater than the sum of their parts.

At the heart of Fusion lies the integration of two critical Factors: Trust and Collaboration and Learning and Innovation. Trust is a driving force that connects individuals, fostering deeper relationships and a collaborative work environment. A focus on Learning supports the drive to discover and grow, creating a culture that drives Innovation. Together, they represent the fusion of people working together, creating energy for new ideas and solutions that drive business growth.

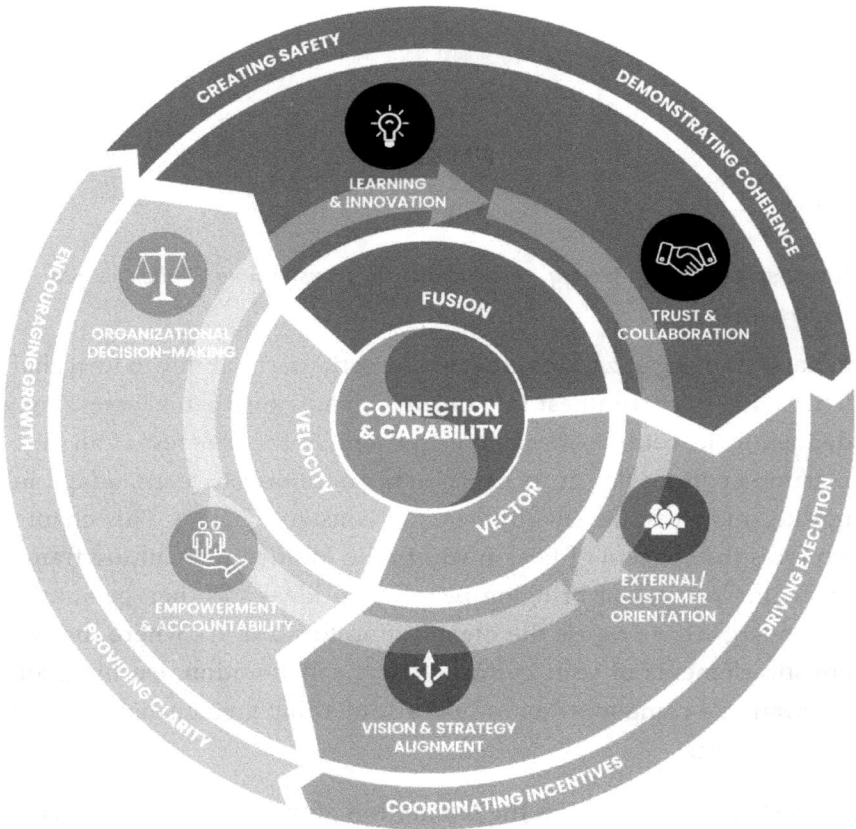

As we move forward, we will delve deeper into the two fundamental components of Fusion: Learning and Innovation, and Trust and Collaboration. These elements are the lifeblood of a dynamic, resilient culture that can withstand and thrive amidst the challenges of a rapidly changing business landscape. Understanding and nurturing these elements within your organization will set the stage for sustained momentum and long-term success.

7

LEARNING

Where the Head Goes, the Body Follows – the Impact of Learning on Culture

Learning precedes action, and actions define your culture – so the head directs the body. When the head turns towards innovative and collaborative learning, the body—comprising your entire workforce—follows with renewed energy and capability. This shift isn't about individual learning; it's about fostering an environment where learning is a collective experience, where humans connect around shared experiences and value creation. When people engage in learning together, they aren't just acquiring new skills, they're building stronger relationships, aligning with the organization's strategic direction, and reinforcing a cohesive culture. In this chapter, we'll focus on the importance of Learning in shaping culture and explore how transforming your approach to learning can ignite a cascade of positive changes, ultimately driving exceptional business results.

Things You Will Learn in This Chapter

- What employees really expect from corporate learning
- The importance of aligning your learning strategy with business outcomes.
- The role of senior leaders in fostering a learning culture.
- Practical steps to create a cultural flywheel with learning and innovation.

The Challenge of Effective Learning

Corporate workplace learning and development (L&D) is a massive $380 billion market globally in 2023, with annual growth of 3-5% over the last 15 years, according to Statista[4]. This translates to roughly $1200 per employee per year. Despite this substantial investment, most business leaders feel they are not seeing meaningful ROI. The reason is simple: we are not investing wisely. Organizations are pouring money into flat, passive learning content that is not meaningfully connected to actions that drive the business. They are operating off the premise that simply introducing new information will change behavior. But if that is the case, no one would ever do anything that was dangerous or bad for them. It is important to remember that;

$$\Delta i \neq \Delta b$$

Or, in non-physics terms, a change in information does not always translate to a change in behavior. The reasons are straightforward. The reality is that passive learning—such as eLearning programs—don't provide the immersive experience needed to change mindsets and drive differentiated actions. In the early 2000s, thought leaders in L&D had already concluded that individually oriented, virtual training delivered little to no impact on business results and were moving towards more experiential approaches to capability development. However, the COVID-19 pandemic pushed us back into the dark ages of the 1990s when we thought CDs, or the internet alone could revolutionize human learning.

While the internet and AI have their place in knowledge transfer, passive learning has been proven to translate poorly into meaningful behavior or actions for several reasons:

- *The Forgetting Curve:* Research shows that people forget approximately 50% of new information within an hour of learning it and up to 70% within 24 hours, if no effort is made to retain it[5].

---

[4] (Statista, 2024)
[5] (Ebbinghaus, 1885)

- *Learning is often positioned as something you must do, not something you get to do:* This compliance-focused approach diminishes engagement and retention.

- *Using inexpensive off-the-shelf eLearning communicates how valued that effort is:* It sends a message that learning isn't a priority.

- *Senior leaders don't lead and demonstrate their learning mindset:* Without visible commitment from the top, a learning culture struggles to take root.

- *Passive learning solutions tend to be non-customized:* This limits the potential to drive change in the skills, processes or behaviors that tangibly impact business value creation.

Behavior is directed by Mindsets (Will Do) and Skills (Can Do). Training that is customized can build non-generic, business-relevant skills. If those training initiatives are also experiential and collaborative in nature, people can experience them in a way that form new mindsets toward the work at hand. So, in a Momentum Culture, the formula is:

$$\Delta E \rightarrow \Delta S + \Delta M \rightarrow \Delta B \rightarrow \Delta R$$

Powerful, Collaborative Learning Experiences → New Collective Mindsets and Skills → Differentiated, Targeted Actions or Behaviors → Improved Business Results.

Momentum Cultures don't value training for the sake of certificates; they expect learning initiatives to deliver tangible results. As mentioned earlier, a "learning culture" should be an investment in learning as a capability, one that builds upon itself and creates asymmetric returns.

Research on the Impact of Learning on Culture

In our research, Learning and Innovation is the second most dominant driver of employee perception of culture, both positively and negatively. When employees believe that the company authentically demonstrates support for learning and building organizational capabilities that truly help them advance their career, they engage with the company culture in a strongly positive way.

The primary driver of employees' perception of the importance of learning and innovation in the enterprise's culture is proven to be the employees' assessment of the quality and usefulness of corporate learning interventions. When people feel that they have a level of agency in their development, and that solutions are tangibly helpful to their career growth, their perception of the culture of learning changes meaningfully. The converse is also true – there is a strong negative perception attached to generic learning tools or compliance-driven learning.

> *"Focus on allowing employees to engage in learning in a way that is in keeping with our workload and day-to-day delivery, rather than things which are designed to look good but aren't meaningful."*

—Research Responses

Contextual perceptions around organizational learning issues vary depending on overall perception of culture. Respondents who are Culture Accelerators - those employees with a positive outlook toward company culture - tend to ask their organization for more training opportunities, and for more collaborative interactions with co-workers. Moreover, they suggest those collaborative learning engagements be focused on key initiatives that drive innovation and business growth. Culture Decelerators- those employees with a more negative outlook toward company culture -tend to express slightly less positive perspectives. They challenge the organization to provide more time to focus on training and for more honest support from managers in that effort. There were several other key insights related to organizational learning uncovered in the research project.

Humans Learn Best from Other Humans

One of the core insights from our research is that humans learn best through interaction and dialogue. This style of learning creates a deeper understanding and important context about how the learning applies to specific issues within the organization. In our interviews, live in-person learning environments were consistently highlighted as powerful culture builders. These settings are more effective in creating relationship bonds and enhancing capabilities compared to isolated learning experiences. While technology has its place, its primary value lies in bringing people together efficiently or enhancing the learning experience. Human-centered learning fosters a collaborative atmosphere that encourages deeper engagement, retention, and application.

Senior Leaders Must Lead by Example

Senior leaders play a crucial role in fostering a learning culture by clarifying how the learning connects to strategy and organizational goals, but also, simply in leading by example. They demonstrate their commitment by actively participating in learning activities and investing in opportunities that bring people together. When leaders visibly engage in learning, it sends a powerful message that learning is valued and essential for growth. While leaders often face challenges in finding time for learning, overcoming these challenges demonstrates learning as a strategic activity and communicates that it is integral part of culture. Leaders must make time for learning and hold themselves and their teams accountable for integrating new knowledge into their daily practices.

Externally Focused Learning Drives Results

Focusing learning efforts on external factors such as customers, markets, and value creation drives the firm toward sustaining competitive advantage by adapting to changing market conditions. On the other hand, training employees on existing internal processes, while important, can tend to reinforce the status quo. By aligning learning with external goals, organizations can drive innovation, improve customer satisfaction, and achieve better business outcomes. The upcoming case study will illustrate how this approach leads to substantial improvements.

CASE EXAMPLE: CHIEF LEARNING OFFICER'S CHALLENGE

In the 2010s, the largest brick-and-mortar retailer in the world had begun to realize that their ability to continue to grow profitability through continuous margin expansion via their supply chain was weakening. They simply were not going to be able to grow margins through one-sided negotiation sustainably. They were going to have to collaborate with their vendor partners to find new efficiencies. To support this initiative, the Chief Learning Officer (CLO) was challenged to create a differentiated learning experience for their executives. The goal was to foster a learning culture that focused externally, engaging with partners to drive shared innovation. My consulting team was tasked with developing a unique executive leadership experience that extended beyond the internal confines of the organization[6].

Innovative Learning Experience

We engaged two of the retailer's largest vendors to create a collaborative executive leadership program, the world's largest soft drink company and a leading personal care consumer packaged goods company. This program combined executives from all three companies in a realistic business simulation. These executives swapped roles, running their partners' companies and facing challenges designed to mirror real-world scenarios. This setup forced them to step into new perspectives, understand their partners' mindsets, and see the interdependencies of the entire ecosystem—from raw materials to the consumer.

---

[6] (Businesswire, 2012)

Outcomes

The executives gained invaluable insights into how their partners created value, leading to more effective collaboration and stronger relationships. One participant commented, "I came here wanting to better understand how your business worked, now I understand how you think".
The program fundamentally changed how these leaders collaborated
externally, resulting in reduced supply chain costs and improved efficiency across the system. The collaboration uncovered new opportunities for innovation and growth that have been leveraged for nearly 15
years. Leaders who participated in the program experienced promotion
rates twice as high as their non-participating peers, and they now run
significant business units within their respective organizations.

Cultural Impact

The impact on culture was profound. The learning experience was
highly sought after, earning industry awards and sparking new conversations between managers and their teams about contributing to business performance. It signaled to employees that their organization was
a place where they could grow as leaders and advance their careers.
The relationships and competencies developed during this program
increased cultural momentum, fostering a thriving, collaborative environment.

LEVERAGE POINTS

- *Invest in Externally Focused Learning:* Learning programs that focus
  on external market dynamics and customer needs drive greater
  innovation and business impact.

- *Create Collaborative Learning Experiences:* Bringing people together to
  learn and solve problems collectively builds stronger relationships
  and more effective teams. Trust can be built through deeper understanding of the mindsets of others.

MAKING THE SHIFT TO A MOMENTUM CULTURE

For Organizations

In a Momentum Culture, the organization is committed to fostering continuous learning and development. It invests in programs that promote lifelong learning, including cross-functional training and leadership development. Cross-functional teams and leadership academies facilitate collaboration and the growth of future leaders. Recognition platforms celebrate employees who actively engage in learning, driving results and innovation. The organization's core values—commitment to growth, recognition of achievement, and sustained excellence—guide all learning initiatives. The organization views its employees as dedicated learners and leaders who contribute to a culture of continuous improvement and collective success.

For Individuals

In a Momentum Culture, employees are committed to continuous learning and personal growth. They proactively seek new knowledge and view challenges as opportunities to enhance their skills and effectiveness. Employees support team learning, fostering a culture of shared knowledge. Adaptability, communication, and resilience are key skills, underpinned by a growth mindset, curiosity, and optimism. Employees feel valued and motivated in an environment that recognizes their efforts, contributing to a culture of innovation and continuous improvement that drives both personal and organizational success.

MOMENTUM CULTURE LEARNING MODEL

Individuals	Organizations
Behaviors	**Processes & Capabilities**
• **Proactively Seeks Knowledge:** Continuously pursues new information, skills, and insights relevant to their role, industry, and customer needs. • **Applies Learning to Work:** Regularly integrates new knowledge and skills into their work to improve processes, products, or services. • **Encourages Team Learning:** Actively fosters a culture of learning within the team, sharing insights and encouraging others to pursue personal and professional growth. • **Embraces Challenges:** Views obstacles as opportunities to learn and grow, approaching challenges with curiosity and a problem-solving mindset.	• **Cross-Functional Training:** Provide opportunities for employees to engage in cross-functional training to broaden their knowledge and apply learning in different contexts. • **Leadership Development Programs:** Establish programs that focus on developing leaders who can mentor and foster a learning culture. • **Collaborative Learning Platforms:** Deploy platforms that facilitate peer-to-peer learning, knowledge sharing, and collaboration. • **Recognition of Learning Efforts:** Develop a system to recognize and reward employees who actively engage in learning and apply their knowledge.
Skills	**Structures & Resources**
• **Adaptability:** Skilled in adjusting to new conditions, learning from experiences, and applying that learning to new situations. • **Communication:** Proficient in clearly sharing knowledge and ideas with others, fostering a collaborative learning environment. • **Resilience:** Maintains focus in the face of challenges, using setbacks as learning opportunities.	• **Cross-Functional Teams:** Structure teams composed of members from different departments to facilitate cross-functional training and knowledge exchange. • **Leadership Academies:** Create dedicated facilities or online platforms focused on leadership development, offering tailored programs and mentoring opportunities. • **Recognition Platforms:** Promote digital platforms or systems that allow peers and leaders to recognize and reward learning efforts in real-time.

Extrinsic

Mindsets	Values
• **Growth Mindset:** I believe that my abilities and intelligence can be developed through dedication and hard work. Learning is a lifelong journey. • **Curiosity:** I believe that there is always more to learn and understand, and I approach the world with a desire to explore new ideas and perspectives. • **Optimism:** I believe that solutions exist for every problem, and I approach the world with a positive outlook that drives me to seek and apply new knowledge. • **Proactivity:** I approach the world with the belief that it is up to me to seek out learning opportunities and not wait for them to come to me.	• **Commitment to Growth:** We believe that continuous learning and development are essential for both individual and organizational success. • **Leadership in Learning:** We believe in developing leaders who inspire and mentor others, fostering a culture of continuous learning. • **Recognition of Achievement:** We believe in acknowledging and celebrating the efforts of those who actively engage in learning and apply their new knowledge. • **Sustained Excellence:** We believe that a commitment to continuous learning leads to sustained excellence in everything we do.

Perception

"I believe I am part of an organization that values continuous growth and learning. In this environment, my curiosity is encouraged, my contributions are valued, and I am empowered to seek out opportunities to develop and apply new knowledge. Challenges are seen as opportunities to innovate and grow, and I am motivated by the belief that there is always a way forward. This culture drives me to proactively engage in my personal and professional development, knowing that my efforts contribute to both my success and the success of the organization."

"We see our employees as dedicated learners who are deeply committed to their personal and professional growth. They actively engage in continuous learning and development, consistently applying new knowledge to their work. We recognize their efforts and celebrate their achievements, knowing that their pursuit of excellence drives our collective success. Our employees are leaders in learning, inspiring and mentoring others, and contributing to a culture of sustained excellence across the organization. Together, we foster an environment where learning is valued, supported, and rewarded, leading to ongoing innovation and growth."

BUILDING YOUR CULTURAL FLYWHEEL

Creating a momentum culture is not just about setting the right values and mindsets, but about embedding these principles into the very fabric of your organization. Here are some thought-provoking questions and tangible steps to help you start building momentum in your culture:

Thought-Provoking Questions:

1. To what degree does your talent development strategy prioritize and provide for collaborative learning initiatives? How are your investments and your people's time being allocated – learning alone or learning together?

2. How closely do your learning programs align with your strategic goals? Are they designed to address the most critical skill areas for creating growth and improved financial returns?

3. To what extent are your learning programs focused on external factors, such as customers, suppliers, and competitors?

4. How do employees perceive the opportunity to participate in your learning programs—excitement and envy (momentum builder) or compliance and contempt (friction)?

5. Do the leaders in your firm devote enough time to mentoring others and fostering a learning environment?

6. How do you recognize and reward leaders and employees for their specific efforts and successes in applying new knowledge and skills?

7. Are you seeing a Flywheel effect from learning investments? Are they cascading widely across the organization? Are they delivering ROI through product/service improvements, new business ideas, improved customer satisfaction, efficiency improvements, better collaboration?

Turning Thought Into Action:

1. Reallocate investment to learning engagements that bring employees together to learn and solve problems for the organization, ensuring immediate ROI.

2. Conduct a thorough review of your current learning programs as to their match with the strategic needs you identified, the enthusiasm of employees to apply what they have learned, and the performance outcomes achieved. Eliminate or redesign learning programs that fall short on those criteria.

3. Include more external, market-driven content in existing, redesigned, and new learning programs

4. Develop processes to identify, reward, and publicly recognize leaders and employees who apply and deliver tangible outcomes from new knowledge.

Resources

I have created a set of companion tools that can help you implement the concepts shared in the book. Here is a link to those tools:

Conclusion

By aligning your learning strategies with business objectives and focusing on creating a supportive, engaging learning culture, you can build a momentum culture that drives continuous improvement and exceptional business results. This chapter has provided insights into how learning can transform your organization, but this is just the beginning. As you move forward, consider how each step you take can contribute to building a cultural flywheel that sustains momentum and propels your organization to new heights.

8
INNOVATION

No Risk it, No Biscuit – How Embracing Risk Drives Innovation and Competitive Advantage

I was consulting for a large construction company, working with their project managers on how to maximize margin and customer satisfaction in their projects. As we delved into strategies for eliminating risk, the CFO stopped me mid-sentence.

> *"Whoa. Stop. We do not want to eliminate risk. If there is no risk, there is no margin. We just need to understand risk better than our competitors and customers."*

His words struck a chord. Risk wasn't something to be feared or avoided—it was an opportunity, a necessary ingredient for growth and profitability.

This insight mirrors the mindset of football coach Bruce Arians, who famously said,

> *"No Risk it, No Biscuit."*

– in other words, no risk, no reward. Arians wasn't content with playing it safe; he coached his teams to lean into risk, seeing it as the path to winning big. The same philosophy applies to business. How does your organization perceive risk? Is it a danger to be mitigated or an opportunity to seize? In this chapter, we'll explore how embracing risk can drive innovation and give your organization a competitive edge. Momentum Cultures are not satisfied with winning their "fair share". They want an "unfair share" of the markets they participate in, and you don't get that without some risk.

Things You Will Learn in This Chapter

- *How to Reframe Risk as an Opportunity:* Understand how a shift in perspective can transform risk from something to avoid into a powerful driver of growth and innovation.

- *The Role of Psychological Safety in Innovation:* Learn how fostering an environment where employees feel safe to take risks and challenge the status quo can lead to better outcomes.

- *Empowering Innovation Through Resources and Training:* Discover why organizations must provide the necessary resources, training, and time to enable employees to innovate effectively.

- *Practical Steps to Build a Risk-Embracing Culture:* Explore strategies to create a culture that encourages risk-taking, continuous learning, and adaptability.

The Challenge of Complacency in Established Organizations

One of the most significant barriers to innovation in established organizations is complacency. This complacency often stems from a natural desire to minimize risk to protect what has already been built—after all, successful companies have much to lose. Organizations that have reached a certain level of success in their industry tend to cling to the status quo, focusing on strategies that ensure business continuity and minimize risk.

While this approach might protect short-term stability, it often leads to a culture where innovation is stifled. The mindset of "if it ain't broke, don't fix it" can prevent companies from recognizing and seizing new opportunities. As a result, any comments or questions that challenge the status quo may be dismissed as "not aligned" or coming from someone who is "not on the bus with us." This resistance to change creates a significant obstacle to growth, especially in dynamic markets where competitors are constantly adapting. To thrive in today's business environment, companies must break free from this complacency, reframe their approach to risk, and embrace innovation as a continuous process of reinvention.

The Tension Between Stability and Adaptation

Focusing on stability and consistency has undeniable advantages. It creates predictability, ensures reliable operations, and helps maintain a company's market position. However, this focus can become a double-edged sword when organizations operate in dynamic markets characterized by constant change.

The more dynamic the industry, the bigger the danger to standing pat. Competitors adapt, and what was once innovative quickly becomes "table stakes", or the basic expectations customers have. What might have seemed too risky to pursue yesterday is often the standard today, and small, seemingly insignificant opportunities can grow into major market trends overnight.

The problem is even more insidious for successful companies. The more successful you are, the more certain you become of your own strategies, and the less you worry about "keeping up with the Joneses" because you start to believe that you are the "Joneses". This sense of certainty can breed complacency, leading organizations to stop learning and making them more susceptible to disruption. Success also brings size, and with size comes the accumulation of assets and resources that are at risk—the bigger the company, the harder the fall. This creates a vicious cycle: as companies grow and succeed, they become more resistant to change, making them even more vulnerable to the very disruptions they dismiss. In such a fast-paced environment, organizations that focus solely on stability can find themselves left behind. The challenge lies in recognizing that stability does not mean standing still—instead, in Momentum Cultures, it is redefined as having the flexibility to adapt, while maintaining core strengths.

Research on the Impact of Innovation on Culture

Our research reveals that how an organization perceives and manages risk is directly linked to its capacity for innovation. Organizations that view risk as something to fear and avoid tend to stagnate, while those that see it as a driver of growth and opportunity are more likely to innovate and thrive. This mindset is crucial not only for fostering a culture of innovation but also for ensuring that the organization remains adaptable in the face of change. The key to success lies in whether the organization actively engages its employees in exploring new ideas and invests in pursuing new areas of growth. Employees want to see their company evolving and adapting at a pace that matches or exceeds the changes happening in the world around them. When they do, their engagement with the company culture is strongly positive. However, when they perceive the company as being complacent, they tend to disengage significantly.

The Positive Impact of Encouraging Experimentation

Respondents with a positive perspective on their company culture often highlight the importance of a safe environment where experimentation is encouraged. These "Culture Accelerators" recognize that their organizations view experimentation as a form of continuous learning, rather than a pass-or-fail test. For example, one respondent noted,

> *"Our company has created a safe environment where employees are encouraged to experiment, take risks, and learn from failures without fear of negative consequences."*

—Research Responses

This approach fosters a culture where employees are more willing to take risks, knowing that their efforts will be valued even if they don't always succeed. Another key insight from Culture Accelerators is the emphasis on external factors. While some organizations focus inwardly, those with a more innovative culture are attuned to market trends and customer needs. They consistently reference customers when discussing innovation, signaling that their approach to innovation is driven by understanding and anticipating customer demands.

The Dangers of Inaction and Lip Service

On the other hand, respondents with a more negative view of their company's culture, "Culture Decelerators", often express frustration with their organization's approach to innovation. These employees report that their organizations talk about innovation but fail to allocate the necessary resources—be it time, money, or training—to make it happen. As one respondent pointed out,

> **"We take risks, but oddly, we don't fully back them; we invest in creation but then skimp on marketing investment."**

—Research Responses

This half-hearted approach to innovation leads to disengagement, as employees feel their efforts are not fully supported. Additionally, Decelerators frequently mention the lack of structured training programs on design thinking and innovation. They express a desire for more training and incentivization for experimentation, suggesting that without these supports, innovation is more likely to flounder, than flourish.

Reframing Risk: Turning Uncertainty into Opportunity

One of the most significant insights from our research is the need to reframe how organizations perceive risk. Momentum Cultures do not see risk as inherently good or bad; it is simply a form of uncertainty. And within that uncertainty lies the potential for asymmetric growth—opportunities that can lead to outsized rewards. These companies understand that by leaning into uncertainty, they can discover new avenues for success that others might overlook. The key is to shift the mindset from fearing risk to embracing it as a catalyst for innovation. This approach requires a cultural shift where employees are encouraged to take calculated risks, knowing that failure is not a disaster but a steppingstone to learning and future success. By fostering an environment where risk is seen as an opportunity, companies can unlock new potential and drive continuous growth.

> *"I wish my company could embrace a culture of experimentation and learning from mistakes."*

—Research Responses

Fostering Innovation Through Collaboration: The Power of Diverse Ideas

Innovation rarely happens in isolation. Instead, it is the product of collaboration, where diverse ideas and perspectives come together to solve complex, "wicked" problems. Our research underscores the importance of fostering a culture of collaboration, where debate and healthy conflict are not just tolerated but encouraged. In these environments, employees are empowered to challenge the status quo, engage in deep discussions, and explore ideas from all angles. This collaborative approach is essential for generating the kind of breakthrough innovation that can set a company apart from its competitors. However, for collaboration to be effective, the organization's culture must support it. This means creating structures and processes that facilitate open communication, cross-functional teamwork, and the free exchange of ideas. When employees feel safe expressing their thoughts, and are encouraged to think creatively, the organization becomes more agile and innovative.

Proactive Innovation: Disrupting Your Own Business Model

In today's fast-paced business environment, waiting for competitors to disrupt your market is a losing strategy. The most successful companies are those that proactively challenge their own business models before others do it for them. This proactive approach to innovation is driven by a deep obsession with understanding customers. By constantly learning about customer needs, preferences, and behaviors, these companies can anticipate changes in the market and adapt before their competitors even realize what's happening. This forward-thinking mindset allows them to "see around corners" and identify emerging trends that can be leveraged for competitive advantage. Moreover, proactive innovation is not just about staying ahead of the competition; it's about continuously evolving the business to meet the ever-changing demands of the market. Companies that embrace this mindset are continuously evolving their businesses to meet the ever-changing demands of the market. Companies that embrace this mindset are better positioned to pivot, capture new opportunities, and ultimately, drive sustainable growth.

CASE EXAMPLE: SHIFTING FROM A DEFENSIVE TO AN OFFENSIVE MINDSET TOWARDS INNOVATION

Challenge

A Fortune 50 global leader in overnight logistics and supply chain management faced a significant challenge as it looked toward the future. Despite its dominant position in the market, the company recognized that its culture around innovation had become increasingly defensive, focused more on protecting its existing assets and maintaining its current business model than on seeking out new opportunities. As a large incumbent with a substantial asset base, company leadership recognized that it was ripe for disruption, and that it needed to transition from a defensive posture to more of an offensive one, particularly among its top executives who were in line for future leadership roles. To achieve this, the Head of Executive Development sought to create a learning experience that would challenge these leaders to think differently, to shift from an internal focus to an external one, take on a more customer-centric approach, and to embrace risk as a necessary component of innovation.

Solution

In response to this challenge, my team and I developed a comprehensive, multi-module program that spanned nearly a year. The program was designed to progressively shift the mindset of these future leaders from self-focused leadership to a broader, more strategic perspective that encompassed their teams, the entire company, and ultimately, the external market.

One of the key components of this program was an immersive learning experience that put the executives in their customers' shoes. We equipped them with classic tools and frameworks associated with Design Thinking, providing them with the context and time to practice and apply these methodologies. This hands-on approach allowed the executives to explore new market opportunities from a fresh perspective, challenging their assumptions and encouraging them to think like disruptors rather than defenders of the status quo.

The culmination of the program was a bold challenge: the executives were tasked with breaking the accepted rules of their industry and identifying ways to disrupt their own business. This exercise pushed them to question deeply ingrained practices and to envision new, innovative paths forward that could position FedEx as a leader in an evolving market.

Outcomes

The results of this program were transformative for both the individuals involved and the company. The executives identified several promising experimental projects for new business offerings that, while risky, had the potential to revolutionize existing service lines. One of these projects evolved into a new line of business that not only complemented but eventually transformed a key service offering, ensuring its relevance in a rapidly changing market.

Cultural Impact

The impact on the executive layer was profound. The emphasis on risk-taking, customer obsession, and innovation became central themes in their leadership approach. The executive development experiences became highly sought after within the company, earning awards and sparking new conversations between managers and their teams about contributing to business performance. It signaled to employees that the company was a place where they could grow as leaders and advance their careers, knowing that their innovative ideas would be valued and supported. The relationships and competencies developed during this program increased cultural momentum, fostering a thriving, collaborative environment where innovation was not just encouraged but expected.

LEVERAGE POINTS

- *No Sacred Cows:* Encourage employees to attack the core assumptions of the business, with no reservation. Reframe this type of ideation from misaligned, to innovative.
- *Customer Obsession:* Almost all market disruptions originate from identifying a customer pain point that was being ignored. Sometimes even the customers themselves are numb to the pain. Only true obsession and intimacy with your customers can help you see the unresolved pain before external forces.

MAKING THE SHIFT TO A MOMENTUM CULTURE OF INNOVATION

For the Organization

In a Momentum Culture, the organization fosters innovation by empowering employees to take risks and explore new ideas. Cross-disciplinary teams and open innovation platforms drive diverse, creative thinking, while leadership actively supports and resources these efforts. Innovation training programs and idea management systems ensure that bold ideas are captured, developed, and rewarded. Core values such as experimentation, support for bold ideas, and customer-centric innovation guide the organization's approach, with agility and flexibility being key to adapting to change. The organization views its employees as fearless innovators who propel the business forward through their creativity and willingness to experiment, driving success in a competitive market.

For Individuals

In a Momentum Culture, employees embrace innovation by taking calculated risks and seeking diverse perspectives. They challenge the status quo, continuously improving processes and products. Creative problem-solving, critical thinking, and adaptability are essential skills, enabling employees to develop innovative solutions and pivot when necessary. Driven by mindsets that embrace uncertainty, openness to change, and a commitment to experimentation, employees feel empowered to explore new ideas and take risks. This culture of innovation fosters both personal growth and organizational success, keeping the organization dynamic and competitive.

MOMENTUM CULTURE MODEL FOR INNOVATION

Individuals	Organizations
Behaviors	**Processes & Capabilities**
Extrinsic • **Embraces Risk-Taking:** Willingly explores unconventional approaches and is open to trying new methods, even if they involve uncertainty. • **Seeks Out Diverse Perspectives:** Actively seeks input and feedback from a variety of sources, including customers, colleagues, and external experts, to fuel innovation. • **Challenges the Status Quo:** Questions existing processes, products, and services, looking for opportunities to improve or revolutionize them.	• **Cross-Disciplinary Teams:** Form teams with members from different disciplines to encourage the exchange of diverse ideas and challenge existing practices. • **Open Innovation Platforms:** Establish platforms that allow employees, partners, and customers to contribute ideas and collaborate on innovative projects. • **Leadership Support for Innovation:** Ensure leaders actively encourage and support innovation, providing the necessary resources and removing barriers. • **Innovation Training Programs:** Provide training programs that equip employees with the skills and mindset needed to innovate effectively.
Skills	**Structures & Resources**
Intrinsic • **Creative Problem-Solving:** Can think outside the box and develop unique solutions to complex challenges. • **Critical Thinking:** Can analyze situations deeply, identify underlying issues, and challenge conventional thinking. • **Adaptability:** Adjusts quickly to new ideas, changing circumstances, and emerging opportunities.	• **Idea Management Systems:** Establish platforms that allow employees to submit, track, and collaborate on innovative ideas, ensuring transparency and accountability. • **Incentive Programs:** Provide financial and non-financial incentives designed to motivate employees to participate in innovation activities. • **Workshops and Bootcamps:** Regularly schedule workshops and bootcamps focused on building innovation skills and fostering a creative mindset.

Mindsets	Values
• **Embrace of Uncertainty:** I believe that uncertainty is an opportunity for creativity and discovery, and I approach the world with a readiness to explore the unknown. • **Openness to Change:** I approach the world with the belief that change is a constant, and I am always ready to adapt and evolve. • **Experimentation:** I believe that trying new things is key to innovation, and I approach the world with a willingness to test and learn from experiences.	• **Commitment to Experimentation:** We value the process of trial and error, recognizing that innovation often comes from taking risks and learning from failure. • **Support for Bold Ideas:** We value bold thinking and are committed to providing the support necessary to bring innovative ideas to life. • **Recognition of Innovators:** We believe in celebrating and rewarding those who push the boundaries and contribute to our culture of innovation. • **Customer-Centric Innovation:** We value innovation that enhances the customer experience and meets the evolving needs of our clients. • **Agility and Flexibility:** We value the ability to adapt quickly to new ideas and changing circumstances, fostering a culture of agility and flexibility.
Perception	"I believe I am part of an organization that values creativity, embraces uncertainty, and encourages experimentation. In this environment, change is seen as an opportunity, and I am empowered to explore new ideas, challenge the status quo, and take calculated risks. This culture drives me to continuously innovate, knowing that my efforts are supported and that learning from experience is integral to our success. Together, we are creating a dynamic and forward-thinking organization that thrives on innovation."	"We see our employees as innovators who embrace uncertainty and are committed to exploring bold new ideas. They are fearless in their pursuit of innovation, willing to experiment and learn from both successes and failures. Our employees are celebrated for their creativity and recognized for pushing the boundaries, consistently delivering innovations that enhance the customer experience and meet the evolving needs of our clients. They are agile and flexible, quickly adapting to new challenges and opportunities, driving our organization forward in a dynamic and competitive market. Together, we cultivate a culture where innovation is not just encouraged but is integral to our success."

BUILDING YOUR CULTURAL FLYWHEEL

Creating a momentum culture that embraces innovation and risk-taking requires setting the right values and mindsets about embedding these principles into the very fabric of your organization. To build a cultural flywheel, you need to ensure that every part of your organization is aligned and moving in the same direction. This requires continuous effort and strategic focus on both intrinsic and extrinsic factors.

Here are some thought-provoking questions and tangible steps to help you start building momentum in your culture:

Thought-Provoking Questions:

1. How well do your current innovation programs align with your strategic goals. Are they keeping you ahead of competitors in meeting changing customer needs?

2. Are your senior leaders consistent in their messaging about risk. Are they encouraging risk-taking and innovation or are they sending mixed signals? Do they listen with open minds when employees challenge the status quo?

3. Do you have systems and processes to enrich your innovation efforts with cross-functional, diverse input and collaboration?

4. Are the skills and behaviors for effective innovation widespread throughout the organization at levels superior to those of competitors?

5. Do your organization's incentive programs incentivize innovation and take the risks of innovation into account?

6. Do you see a flywheel effect in your innovation programs? Are visible internally and externally, generating enough buzz, and being adopted widely.

7. Are you seeing tangible outcomes from your innovation initiatives—new business ideas, improved customer satisfaction, efficiency improvements, better collaboration?

Turning Thought Into Action:

1. *Evaluate current investments in innovation and development:* What yield are you getting on those investments? Conduct a thorough review of your innovation programs and their outcomes. Identify areas where investments are yielding high returns and areas that need improvement.

2. *Evaluate the focus of current programs and initiatives:* Are they focused on opportunities directly tied to improving critical business capabilities and outcomes.

3. *Retarget your learning opportunities to focus on external markets, not internal processes:* Understanding customer needs and market trends can lead to innovative solutions and better business performance.

Resources

I have created a set of companion tools that can help you implement the concepts shared in the book. Here is a link to those tools:

Conclusion

When that CFO remarked, "We just want to understand risk better than our competitors and customers," he wasn't just talking about mitigating threats, he was pointing to the essence of strategic innovation. The goal isn't to sidestep uncertainty, but to navigate it more skillfully than anyone else. Throughout this chapter, we've explored how this mindset, captured in the "No Risk it, No Biscuit" philosophy, can transform your organization. Embracing risk isn't about reckless gambling; it's about fostering a culture where calculated risks lead to meaningful innovation and sustained competitive advantage.

In the next chapter, we'll explore the crucial role that trust plays in building a resilient, high-performing culture. We'll examine how trust not only fosters innovation but also enables effective collaboration, leading to a powerful culture that can deliver sustained business momentum over time.

9

TRUST

Lack of Trust is the Tax You Pay That You Never Voted For

Organizational trust can either be a tax or a dividend. Research by Paul J. Zak has shown that employees in high-trust organizations are 50% more productive, 76% more engaged, experience 106% more energy at work, and have 40% less burnout compared to those in low-trust organizations[7]. Steven M.R. Covey, in his book The Speed of Trust, emphasizes how trust is the cornerstone of any successful organization, enabling speed and reducing costs[8]. Trust is the fuel that drives Momentum Cultures. Without it, the gears of your organization grind to a halt. Whether employees trust each other, their managers, or the organization, that trust—or the lack thereof—has a profound impact on culture and directly correlates to business success, growth, and profitability.

Things You Will Learn in This Chapter

- How to identify the presence (or absence) of trust within your organization.

- The visible signs and behaviors that indicate strong or weak trust.

- The direct connection between trust and business results, including productivity, profitability, and employee engagement.

- Practical strategies to build and maintain trust within your team and across your organization.

Trust Drives the Bottom Line

Trust is the internal cohesion and mutual respect that exists between team members and between the team and the organization. It is a deep-

---

[7] (Zak, 2017)
[8] (Covey S. M., 2006)

ly human issue, created and destroyed by the actions and behaviors of individuals. Trust is built over time through consistency—trust equals time multiplied by consistency. Time, in this context, refers to the minutes spent together and to the working relationship's overall duration. Consistency refers to the alignment of words and actions, the "do what you say you will do" (DWYSYWD) principle.

The shift to remote and hybrid work environments has significantly challenged trust-building. While the amount of communication within teams has increased, albeit asynchronously, communication across teams has diminished across the board[9]. The lack of physical proximity has made it more difficult to build the trust and connections that are essential for effective collaboration. Organizations must be intentional about creating opportunities for employees to connect, whether in person or through other means, to build and maintain trust.

Trust Erosion is Insidious

Complicating the matter is the fact that trust erosion is often subtle and goes unnoticed until it manifests into significant problems. There is no "Trust-o-meter" to alert organizations to the issue. However, the impact of trust—or the lack thereof—is evident in various aspects of organizational performance.

When trust is low, the organization pays a tax in the form of slower decision-making, inefficient collaboration, and a reluctance to take ownership of projects. On the other hand, when trust is high, the organization reaps a dividend. There tends to be fewer and more productive meetings, alignment comes easily, and employees readily take ownership of action items. Decisions are made quickly, and accountability is embraced. Trust is a silent driver of these positive outcomes, just as its absence underpins the negative ones.

[9] (Zak, 2017)

CASE EXAMPLE: SCHNEIDER DOWNS

Over time, people learn to trust when leaders consistently walk the talk. Ted Pettko, a shareholder of Schneider Downs in Pittsburgh, PA, recalls his early career at a firm where employees were treated as mere cogs in the machine, expected to produce 60 hours of work a week or risk losing their jobs. Despite the occasional pizza as a "reward", the dissonance between the firm's harsh demands and its espoused values of Teamwork and Care destroyed trust. Employees, treated as machines, felt no connection with the company and saw it only as a paycheck provider.

In contrast, Pettko makes sure Schneider Downs is committed to fostering a culture of care, where employees are valued as individuals, not just for their output. In working with Schneider Downs, I can personally attest that this culture of care is palpable, permeating the organization and creating an environment where trust can flourish.

Research on the Impact of Trust on Culture

The Great Place to Work Institute, which partners with Fortune to produce the "100 Best Companies to Work For" list, found that trust between managers and employees is the primary defining characteristic of the very best workplaces. These companies outperform the average annualized returns of the S&P 500 by a factor of three[10]. Similarly, Trust Across America has shown that America's most trustworthy companies consistently outperform the S&P 500, and a 2015 study by Interaction Associates found that high-trust companies are more than 2½ times more likely to be high-performing revenue organizations than low-trust companies[11].

Our research into trust echoes these findings. Trust and collaboration are the top connection factors influencing perceptions of culture effectiveness, surpassing even the relationship with one's manager. This

[10] (Covey S. M., 2016)
[11] (Conant, 2020)

suggests that the organization must be trustworthy before employees can trust each other enough to collaborate effectively. In the Momentum Culture Framework, trustworthiness is created primarily by demonstrating competence (the belief that the organization can follow through on its promises) and coherence (alignment between words and actions). Demonstrating balance in how well an organization treats its entire ecosystem; employees, customers, shareholders, etc. – a visible expression of competence and coherence - is proven to be the biggest driver of whether employees believe they have an environment conducive to collaboration.

> *"The best change would be an emphasis on listening to the concerns of all staff members and functions of the business to build unity as an organization. "*
> —Research Responses

Competence is a Big Part of the Trust Equation

Competence, or the belief that one's colleagues and the organization can follow through on their commitments, is a critical component of trust. When one function or team has weak capabilities, coworkers lose trust in them, begin to work around them, and collaboration breaks down. If this situation persists, employees lose faith in the organization, shifting from a sense of "we are misfiring" to a more destructive mindset of "they are a mess." This can lead to self-protective behaviors that are the antithesis of a high-performing culture. For trust to thrive, competence must be continuously expected, developed and reinforced across the organization.

Coherency: The Foundation of Trust

Coherency is the alignment between what the organization and its leaders say and what they do. Values are powerful, but they are meaningless—or even harmful—if not backed by consistent actions. Momentum Cultures take the time to contextualize their values, translating them into tangible behaviors and clearly defining what those behaviors look like in practice. For example, if a company values transparency, leaders must consistently demonstrate this by openly sharing information, even when it's difficult. When there is a gap between stated values and actual behaviors, it creates dissonance, erodes trust, and undermines the culture.

Trust is Built by Collaboration

Trust does not happen in isolation; it is built through collaboration. People are more likely to trust those they know and have worked with closely. This is particularly challenging in remote and hybrid work environments, where opportunities for personal interaction are limited. Organizations must find ways to bring people together to work on challenging problems as a team. These collaborative efforts build personal connections and relationships, which are the foundation of a strong culture. Interestingly, the research indicates that a great culture is often characterized by the sentiment that "working hard at big challenges with my co-workers is actually fun." This sense of camaraderie and mutual support is a hallmark of high-trust environments. Making things easy is not the same as fostering a positive culture—in fact, the opposite may be true. Many of the individuals I interviewed shared stories of doing the hardest work of their lives, but because they loved their coworkers and trusted them, it was the best culture they had ever experienced.

CASE EXAMPLE: HIGH-TECH SITE CONSTRUCTION COMPANY

Challenge

A large engineering, procurement, and construction company focused on high-tech manufacturing faced significant challenges due to a lack of trust both internally and externally. Initially, the company believed that the issue lay with ineffective project managers who needed better training to improve their management skills. However, as my team delved deeper into the collaborative dynamics across various functions, we discovered that the underlying issue was simply a pervasive lack of trust.

Project managers did not trust procurement to deliver materials on time, leading them to request more than they needed, which strained the system. Project managers also held back contingency funds until the very end of projects, negatively impacting cash flow and forcing the finance team to expand credit lines unnecessarily. Senior leadership's lack of trust in the competence of project managers further slowed decision-making, impacting project schedules and leading to customer dissatisfaction.

The mistrust extended to the finance team, which constrained project managers' access to funds to manage profitability, further straining relationships. This lack of trust led to a vicious cycle where each function tried to protect itself at the expense of the whole, directly impacting the company's profitability.

The trust issues at the firm had far-reaching consequences. The lack of internal trust not only impaired collaboration and decision-making but also increased capital requirements, leading to higher costs of capital. Trust, or the lack thereof, is like a virus—it spreads quickly from one stakeholder to another, and there is no easy vaccine. In this case, the erosion of trust was costly, both financially and in terms of the company's culture and reputation.

Solution

The CFO challenged my team to create a development experience for their Project Managers to build business acumen and general project management skills like forecasting, stakeholder management, driving profitability, etc. While the experience delivered on all these stated goals, it also uncovered these issues of trust. When we debriefed with company leadership at the insights we found, we made a major pivot. We didn't change the experience, we changed who participated.

Instead of just project managers, we included superintendents, project accountants, procurement, and a whole slate of functions that all contributed to overall project success. Each simulation team included cross-functional leaders, challenging these disparate roles to come together to optimize project performance.

These types of challenges are common throughout the EPC industry. Project success is defined by a delicate balance of very different metrics. Profitability is critical and obvious, but given the narrow margins of the business, capital efficiency can be just as important in many projects. But creating success with a wide range of stakeholders – the buying customer, the construction labor (who are always in tight demand), the internal employees, and even the local communities is dependent upon a set of high-trust relationships.

Outcome

Project profitability rose across the board, but creating success with stakeholders is where the company really found value, and that came from increased trust. All employees – both in the field and in the home office – now had a higher level of trust with one another and gained a common language and approach to decisions. With a deeper understanding of the interdependencies of each contribution to overall project success, collaboration improved drastically, resulting in more profitable projects, happier customers, and more engaged employees.

LEVERAGE POINTS:

- Weak execution is commonly attributed to poor skills or commitment, but it can often be traced back to trust problems. In 1:1s, probe for the level of trust between working partners.

MAKING THE SHIFT TO A MOMENTUM CULTURE OF TRUST

For the Organization

In a Momentum Culture, the organization is committed to fostering trust at every level. It invests in capabilities like open communication channels, leadership modeling, and conflict resolution systems to promote transparency, integrity, and collaboration. Internal communication platforms, leadership training, and transparency dashboards support these efforts, ensuring employees are informed and engaged. Rotational programs and on-site collaboration hubs further enhance cross-functional trust. The organization's core values of integrity, transparency, and consistency guide all actions, with employees seen as reliable, open, and key contributors to a culture of trust. Trust is foundational to the organization's success, and every employee plays a vital role in sustaining it.

For Individuals

In a Momentum Culture, trust is the foundation of all relationships. Employees consistently demonstrate integrity, acting with honesty and ethical principles that build trust with colleagues and leaders. Open communication fosters collaboration and mutual respect, while individuals take responsibility for mistakes, reinforcing trust and accountability. Emotional intelligence, active listening, and interpersonal communication are crucial skills that support a trusting environment. Guided by integrity, empathy, and transparency, employees contribute to a cohesive, trust-based workplace. They feel encouraged to communicate openly and work together effectively, knowing that trust is key to their collective success and a positive work environment.

MOMENTUM CULTURE MODEL FOR TRUST

	Individuals	Organizations
	Behaviors	**Processes & Capabilities**
Extrinsic	• **Demonstrates Integrity:** Consistently acts with honesty and transparency, keeping commitments and upholding ethical standards. • **Communicates Openly:** Shares information transparently and honestly, fostering an environment of trust through clear and direct communication. • **Admits Mistakes:** Takes responsibility for errors and openly discusses them, using them as opportunities to learn and build trust. • **Seeks to Understand:** Takes the time to understand others' perspectives, fostering trust by showing empathy and consideration.	• **Open Communication Channels:** Establish formal and informal channels for transparent communication at all levels of the organization, fostering an environment of openness and honesty. • **Leadership Modeling:** Ensure that leaders consistently model the behavior of admitting mistakes and taking responsibility, setting a strong example for all employees. • **Conflict Resolution Systems:** Develop systems that provide employees with the tools and support needed to address and resolve conflicts in a way that fosters trust and understanding. • **Cross-Functional Collaboration Initiatives:** Create initiatives that encourage collaboration between different departments, fostering trust through shared goals and mutual understanding.

Skills	Structures & Resources
• **Emotional Intelligence:** Is able to recognize, understand, and manage one's own emotions, as well as to empathize with others. • **Active Listening:** Can fully concentrate on, understand, and respond thoughtfully to what others are saying. • **Interpersonal Communication:** Is proficient in clearly and effectively conveying ideas and information in one-on-one and group settings.	• **Internal Communication Platforms:** Provide tools such as intranets, Slack, or Microsoft Teams that facilitate open and transparent communication across the organization. • **Leadership Training Programs:** rain leaders on how to model integrity, openness, and accountability in their daily interactions. • **Transparency Dashboards:** Provide tools that offer visibility into key decisions, company performance, and strategic initiatives, ensuring transparency and inclusiveness in decision-making. • **Rotational Programs:** Rotate employees through different departments, providing them with broader organizational knowledge and fostering cross-functional trust. • **On-Site Collaboration Hubs:** Physical spaces equipped with tools and technology to support collaborative work, where teams can gather to brainstorm and solve problems together.

Mindsets	Values
• **Integrity:** I believe that honesty and transparency are the foundations of trust, and I approach the world with a commitment to ethical behavior. • **Empathy:** I believe that understanding others' perspectives is key to building trust, and I approach the world with a commitment to empathetic listening. • **Transparency:** I believe that being open about my intentions and actions fosters trust, and I approach the world with a commitment to transparency.	• **Integrity:** We believe that honesty and transparency are the foundations of trust, and we are committed to upholding the highest ethical standards. • **Transparency:** We value open and clear communication, ensuring that all decisions and actions are made with transparency and inclusiveness. • **Consistency:** We believe that consistency in actions and decisions is crucial for maintaining trust within the organization.

Intrinsic

<table>
<tr>
<td rowspan="2">Perception</td>
<td>"I believe I am part of an organization that values honesty, and transparency. In this environment, trust is built through open communication, ethical behavior, and a genuine commitment to understanding others. I feel empowered to admit mistakes, learn from them, and approach every interaction with empathy and integrity. This culture fosters strong, trust-based relationships, where everyone feels respected and supported, and where transparency is the norm. Together, we create a trustworthy and reliable organization that values each person's contribution."</td>
<td>"We see our employees as individuals who embody integrity, consistently acting with honesty and transparency in their work. They communicate openly and take responsibility for their actions, building trust through their reliability and consistency. Through their collaborative efforts, they foster a culture of trust and mutual respect, working together to achieve our shared goals. Together, we create an environment where trust is not just encouraged but is foundational to everything we do."</td>
</tr>
</table>

BUILDING YOUR CULTURAL FLYWHEEL

Creating a momentum culture is about embedding these principles into every aspect of your organization. The goal is to align your organization so that every part is moving in unison, creating a self-sustaining cycle of trust, collaboration, and continuous improvement. To build a cultural flywheel that accelerates and sustains momentum, you need to focus on both intrinsic and extrinsic factors, ensuring that trust is a foundational element of your organizational culture.

Thought-Provoking Questions:

1. Consider how information is currently shared. Are there opportunities to make decision-making processes more transparent? Would sharing more about the company's direction, financial health, and strategic initiatives help build trust among employees?

2. Evaluate the communication practices of your leadership team. Are they regularly engaging with employees in a way that builds trust? Could more frequent or more open communication help foster a stronger connection between leaders and their teams?

3. Think about the goals and KPIs set for your teams. Are they aligned in a way that fosters collaboration, or do they unintention-

ally create silos? How can you adjust these metrics to ensure that everyone is working toward the same objectives and reinforcing trust in the process?

4. Reflect on the level of trust you have in your team's abilities. Are there areas where you feel the need to micromanage? What would it take for you to feel comfortable delegating more responsibility and trusting your team to make decisions independently?

Turning Thought into Action:

- *Bring Your Team Together:* Invest in Co-Location. Even in a remote or hybrid work environment, finding ways to bring your team together in person can significantly build trust. Whether through regular team retreats, co-working days, or strategic offsites, physical proximity fosters stronger relationships and trust that's difficult to replicate online.

- *Require Consistent 1:1s Between Leaders and Direct Reports.* Make regular, meaningful one-on-one meetings a non-negotiable practice, with the goal of face-to-face engagements. These interactions should go beyond surface-level check-ins and delve into the heart of issues, providing a platform for open communication and trust-building. Encourage leaders to actively listen, provide feedback, and show genuine interest in their team members' growth and well-being.

- *Create Structured Opportunities for Leaders to Demonstrate Stated Values.* Develop programs or initiatives that allow leaders to visibly demonstrate the organization's values. Whether through public recognition of aligned behaviors, transparent decision-making, or leading by example in challenging situations, these actions will reinforce trust and the credibility of the organization's values.

Resources

I have created a set of companion tools that can help you implement the concepts shared in the book. Here is a link to those tools:

Conclusion

Trust is one of the most powerful currencies within an organization. It can either levy a heavy tax or pay out a substantial dividend. Moreover, high organizational trust is a competitive edge that is difficult for competitors to replicate. It manifests in numerous ways, from reduced turnover costs due to strong employee retention, to higher productivity because of engaged and motivated employees. Trust impacts every line of the income statement—from reducing the costs of poor retention and engagement to enhancing the quality of output because employees care deeply about their work and the organization.

As we transition to the next chapter on Collaboration, remember that trust is the foundation upon which all effective collaboration is built. But trust doesn't just appear; it must be cultivated, nurtured, and protected. How can your organization foster the trust needed to collaborate effectively and achieve exceptional business results?

COLLABORATION

Culture and the Hidden Costs of Poor Collaboration

Collaboration within an organization is often considered an intangible asset—valued, yet difficult to quantify. However, when collaboration falters, its impact becomes glaringly visible in places few anticipate: your financial statements. The true cost of poor collaboration isn't just inefficiency or frustration; it's a measurable drain on financial performance. Projects slow down, decision-making grinds to a halt, and the organization loses its competitive edge. This isn't just a matter of working together; it's about aligning teams towards a common goal, building trust, and ensuring that every function moves in harmony. As we delve into this chapter, we'll uncover how the undercurrents of poor collaboration can silently erode the foundation of your business and how addressing these hidden costs is essential for sustaining momentum and driving growth.

Things You Will Learn in This Chapter

- *Collaboration vs. Compromise:* Understanding the difference between true collaboration, which leads to win-win outcomes, and compromise, which often results in lose-lose situations. You'll learn why collaboration is more than just coming to an agreement—it's about creating solutions that benefit all parties involved while staying aligned with the organization's goals.

- *Clarity of the "Main Thing":* How having a clear and unified vision or "Main Thing" enables more effective collaboration across teams. We'll explore why clarity around the organization's primary goals simplifies decision-making, reduces friction, and enhances collaborative efforts.

- *Impact of Remote and Hybrid Working Environments:* An examination of how remote and hybrid work setups can hinder collaboration, leading to increased feelings of isolation, miscommunication, and ultimately, a decline in overall effectiveness. This section will provide insights into overcoming these challenges to maintain strong collaborative ties within the organization.

- *The Critical Role of Connection in Trust and Collaboration:* Discover how the fundamental human need for connection is essential in building trust and fostering collaboration. We'll delve into the relationship between trust, collaboration, and the financial performance of an organization, showing how strong connections can be a catalyst for better business outcomes.

Clarity of the Main Thing

Collaboration within organizations is often spoken about, but its true nature and implications are not always fully understood. In a corporate setting, collaboration is not merely about working together; it is about bringing together diverse groups that may have different success metrics or goals and aligning them towards a common objective. When everyone in the organization is fully aligned, it simply becomes teamwork.

The essence of collaboration lies in creating win-win scenarios, where all parties feel they are contributing towards and benefiting from the outcome. This contrasts sharply with compromise, which often leaves all parties involved feeling they have given up something valuable, leading to a lose-lose situation. Compromise can be seen as a sub-optimal solution, where neither side fully achieves their goals, and where the satisfaction and morale of the participants can suffer as a result. Moreover, many people tend to view compromise as capitulation, which breeds resentment.

Momentum Cultures excel at collaboration because they possess a clear vision and strategy, and all team members understand who the "hero" is—whether it's the customer, the company's mission, or a shared objective. This clarity provides a "Main Thing" that helps all collaborating parties align their efforts. Without this clarity, collaboration can devolve into a struggle where each party pulls in a different direction, leading to inefficiency and frustration.

The Changing Environment of Work

Collaboration becomes even more complex in environments where remote and hybrid work setups are prevalent. The rise of remote and hybrid working environments has brought about significant changes in how collaboration is managed within organizations. While these flexible work setups have provided many benefits, including improved work-life balance and increased productivity for some, they have also introduced new challenges that can complicate effective collaboration. The physical separation of team members can lead to isolation, less cross-functional collaboration, and a transactional approach to work, all of which undermine the collaborative spirit.

For many employees, remote work has led to feelings of isolation and disconnection from their colleagues. According to research by Zippia[12], in 2022, 50% of remote employees experienced loneliness at least once per week, and 19% identified isolation as their number one problem at work. Moreover, 70% reported feeling left out of their workplace. These statistics highlight a growing issue—when employees feel disconnected from their peers, their ability to collaborate effectively diminishes.

Further research by Microsoft[13], involving a study of 61,000 of its employees, found that firm-wide remote work led to the collaboration networks of workers becoming more static and siloed, with fewer bridges between disparate parts of the organization. This silo effect hampers cross-functional collaboration, leading to slower decision-making, reduced innovation, and a decline in overall organizational agility.

---

[12] (Zippia, n.d.)
[13] (Microsoft, 2021)

For many employees, the aspiration for a great workplace culture is rooted in a deep-seated need for human connection. Without the spontaneous interactions and informal conversations that naturally occur in a shared physical workspace, remote workers can become overly focused on task completion rather than building relationships. This shift from relational to transactional interactions can undermine trust, which is the foundation of effective collaboration.

The complexities introduced by remote and hybrid work environments necessitate a more intentional approach to fostering collaboration. Organizations must recognize that while technology enables remote work, it does not replace the human elements of trust, connection, and mutual understanding that are critical to successful collaboration. Without addressing these challenges, organizations may find that poor collaboration becomes a hidden cost that eventually shows up on their financial statements in the form of inefficiencies, increased turnover, and lost opportunities.

RESEARCH ON THE IMPACT OF COLLABORATION ON CULTURE

Our research into organizational collaboration reveals some striking insights about how interconnected this concept is with trust, employee engagement, and ultimately, business outcomes. The data underscores the critical importance of human connection in fostering effective collaboration, particularly in the context of remote and hybrid work environments. Let's explore the key findings that emerged from our analysis.

First and foremost, our research highlights the central role of strong, interpersonal bonds in facilitating collaboration. Employees who reported feeling a strong bond with many of their coworkers were significantly more likely to collaborate effectively. This connection fosters trust, which in turn smooths communication and accelerates decision-making. However, the shift to remote and hybrid work has fundamentally altered these relationships for many employees, particularly those who joined their organizations after the onset of COVID-19. These workers often find their work relationships reduced to mere transactional exchanges, lacking the depth and mutual understanding that comes from regular, face-to-face interaction.

Without these foundational relationships, trust becomes tenuous. This erosion of trust leads to miscommunications—where a well-meaning email or Slack message can be misinterpreted—and generates uncertainty about colleagues' intentions. The absence of strong personal connections also makes it harder for employees to gauge the motivations behind feedback or decisions, which can slow down or even derail collaborative efforts. In high-performing organizations, however, there is typically a pervasive understanding of what the "main thing" is—the overarching goal or purpose that guides all efforts. This clarity helps maintain focus and alignment, making collaboration more straightforward and effective.

Culture Accelerators often emphasize the desire for connection and the opportunity to collaborate across units and functions toward meaningful goals. These employees frequently ask for more transparency, asking questions like, "What are we working toward?" and expressing a desire to see the organization allocate time and resources for collaborative efforts. This indicates a strong cultural alignment where employees are eager to engage with the organization's broader mission.

> *"Try to unite more departments. I feel sometimes that we are separated from one another."*
>
> —Research Responses

On the flip side, Culture Decelerators often express concerns about the organization's lack of trust in their productivity, particularly regarding the push to return to the office. They advocate for greater flexibility and autonomy in their work processes, seeing these as key drivers of productivity rather than the physical presence in the office. This perspective highlights a disconnect between employee needs and organizational expectations, which can further exacerbate issues of trust and collaboration.

These findings collectively demonstrate that effective collaboration is not just about having the right tools or processes in place; it's about fostering a culture where trust and connection are prioritized. Momentum Cultures, as we define them, excel in this area because they maintain a clear focus on their "Main Thing," which serves as a unifying force that simplifies collaboration. When employees are aligned around a shared purpose and feel connected to their colleagues, collaboration becomes not just possible, but a natural and productive part of their work.

CASE EXAMPLE – AUTO PARTS MANUFACTURING

Challenge

Several years ago, my team was engaged by a leading auto parts manufacturer for both OEMs and the aftermarket. The company's success depended heavily on its ability to deliver products quickly and reliably—something their customers had come to expect and rely on. However, managing inventory efficiently was also crucial because of the high costs associated with maintaining large stockpiles. This created an ongoing internal struggle: sales teams wanted to keep ample inventory to ensure customer satisfaction, while product marketing aimed to provide accurate forecasts to manufacturing, finance was focused on minimizing the cost of working capital, and the supply chain was tasked with delivering just-in-time.

Each of these departments began to operate in silos, adjusting their communication and actions to optimize their departmental outcomes rather than the customers' and the company's overall success. The sales department inflated forecasts to secure more inventory, product marketing underreported to avoid missed targets, and manufacturing overordered raw materials to prevent downtime, which increased costs and decreased efficiency. This misalignment led to a downward spiral: delivery times worsened, working capital ballooned, and trust between departments eroded. Each department started blaming the others for failures, and collaboration became virtually nonexistent, contributing to significant inefficiencies that impacted the company's financial health.

Solution

Recognizing that the root cause of these issues was ineffective collaboration, the CFO challenged us to help them resolve the issues that were hampering execution and efficiency. To do that, we designed a tailored supply chain simulation for the company. This simulation closely mirrored their actual internal processes, bringing together all the key functional departments—sales, product marketing, manufacturing, finance, and supply chain—for a team-based experience.

In the simulation, teams composed of representatives from each department were challenged to run the company through multiple operating periods, encountering the same bottlenecks and conflicts they experienced in real life. However, this time, they had the opportunity to see these challenges from each other's perspectives and work together to find solutions. The simulation highlighted the importance of collaboration and provided a safe space for employees to experiment with different strategies and approaches without real-world consequences.

Outcomes

The impact of this simulation was profound. As a result of the exercise, the teams fundamentally changed how they communicated and collaborated. They increased the frequency of their communication, but more importantly, they improved its substance—ensuring that it was purpose-driven and aligned with the company's goals. By better understanding each other's success metrics and challenges, the departments began to work together more effectively, aligning around the company's prioritization of customer satisfaction while simultaneously managing working capital more efficiently.

Within just six months, the company saw remarkable improvements: delivery times improved by 17%, and working capital was reduced by 19%, all without the need for additional capital or headcount. These gains were achieved not through complex new processes or technologies, but through improved collaboration driven by trust, clear communication, and a unified focus on the company's "main thing." This case demonstrates how seemingly invisible issues like poor collaboration can have significant financial implications that manifest on the balance sheet but can be effectively addressed through intentional cultural interventions.

LEVERAGE POINTS:

- The more efficient your company gets, the more siloed the functions can get. Invest the time and resources to bring cross-functional groups together to build mutual understanding and improved alignment. Better connected teams create better outcomes.

- The cost of poor collaboration can show up in unexpected places, like inflated working capital, slow cash conversion cycle, and reduced gross margins. These issues are always multi-factorial and usually cross functions, and improved collaboration is always the place to start.

MAKING THE SHIFT TO A MOMENTUM CULTURE OF COLLABORATION

For Organizations:

Making the shift to a Momentum Culture of Collaboration requires organizations to embed collaboration into the core of their operations. This involves creating transparent processes, investing in cross-functional capabilities, and ensuring that structures like collaborative platforms and team-based challenges are in place to foster unity and shared accountability. Leadership must prioritize aligning all departments towards common goals, building trust through mutual respect, and ensuring that collaboration becomes a strategic advantage, driving the organization's mission forward with collective purpose.

For Individuals:

For individuals, transitioning to a Momentum Culture of Collaboration means embracing a mindset focused on collective success and trust-worthiness. It requires consistently aligning personal efforts with team goals, actively engaging in clear and transparent communication, and prioritizing win-win outcomes in every interaction. Individuals must also develop interpersonal skills and a commitment to mutual respect, recognizing that their contributions are essential to the organization's overall success and that true collaboration strengthens both the team and the individual.

MOMENTUM CULTURE MODEL FOR COLLABORATION

	Individuals	Organizations
	Behaviors	**Processes & Capabilities**
Extrinsic	• **Aligns with Common Goals:** Consistently works towards the organization's objectives, ensuring personal and team efforts are aligned with the broader mission. • **Communicates Clearly and Transparently:** Shares information openly and clearly, ensuring that everyone is informed and aligned. • **Balances All Stakeholder Needs:** Considers the needs of all stakeholders when making decisions, aiming for solutions that benefit everyone involved. • **Facilitates Win-Win Solutions:** Actively seeks to create solutions that benefit all parties, ensuring collaborative efforts lead to positive outcomes for everyone.	• **Cross-Functional Collaboration Platforms:** Implement platforms that encourage and support cross-functional collaboration, enabling teams to work together towards shared goals. • **Balanced Scorecard Systems:** Develop systems that track and balance performance metrics across different stakeholders, ensuring that all needs are considered in decision-making. • **Organizational Transparency Initiatives:** Promote transparency throughout the organization by providing visibility into decisions, processes, and outcomes, thereby fostering trust and collaboration.

	Skills	Structures & Resources
Intrinsic	• **Interpersonal Communication:** Is skilled in clearly and effectively conveying ideas and information in collaborative settings. • **Stakeholder Management:** Is able to identify, understand, and manage the needs of different stakeholders in collaborative projects. • **Conflict Resolution:** Can navigate and resolve conflicts in a way that strengthens relationships and enhances collaboration. • **Relationship Building:** Is proficient in developing and maintaining strong, trust-based relationships with colleagues and stakeholders.	• **Stakeholder Experience Simulations:** Provide training environments where teams can simulate the experience of different stakeholders, helping them understand and balance varying needs in collaborative projects. • **Cross-Functional Collaboration Lounges:** Create informal physical spaces within the workplace designed to encourage spontaneous interactions and brainstorming sessions among employees from different departments. • **Cross-Departmental Rotations:** Programs where employees spend time working in different departments, gaining a deeper understanding of other teams' functions and fostering collaboration. • **Team-Based Challenges:** Implement competitive or cooperative challenges designed to build trust, improve communication, and align goals across different teams. • **In-Person Town Halls:** Conduct regular, organization-wide meetings where employees from all levels come together to discuss company goals, share progress, and foster a sense of unity and collective purpose.

Mindsets	Values
• **Collective Success:** I believe that the success of the team is more important than individual achievements, and I approach the world with a focus on shared goals. • **Trustworthiness:** I believe that being consistent and reliable is crucial for building trust, and I approach the world with a commitment to being dependable. • **Collaboration Over Compromise:** I believe that true collaboration creates win-win solutions, and I approach the world with a focus on finding mutually beneficial outcomes rather than settling for compromise.	• **Unity of Purpose:** We believe in aligning all teams and departments with a common mission and goals, ensuring that our collaborative efforts are focused and effective. • **Mutual Respect:** We believe that respect for each other's roles, expertise, and contributions is fundamental to successful collaboration. • **Shared Accountability:** We believe that accountability for results is shared across teams, ensuring that everyone is invested in the success of our collaborative efforts.

Perception

"I perceive my organization as a place where collaboration is not just encouraged but embedded in everything we do. Here, the success of the team takes precedence over individual achievements, and there is a clear commitment to open and transparent communication. I trust that my colleagues and leaders are dependable, and I feel confident that we can find win-win solutions together. The organization supports my growth in building strong relationships, managing stakeholder needs, and resolving conflicts, making it a place where true collaboration thrives."

"We believe in fostering a collaborative environment where cross-functional teams work together seamlessly towards shared goals. Our processes and capabilities are designed to support transparency, mutual understanding, and alignment across all levels of the organization. We invest in resources like cross-departmental rotations and collaboration platforms to enhance teamwork and innovation. Our values of unity of purpose, mutual respect, and shared accountability drive us to maintain a culture where every team member is empowered, respected, and committed to collective success."

BUILDING YOUR CULTURAL FLYWHEEL

Creating a momentum culture is not just about setting the right values and mindsets, but about embedding these principles into the very fabric of your organization. Here are some thought-provoking questions and tangible steps to help you start building momentum in your culture:

Thought-Provoking Questions

1. Consider whether your organization's decision-making is influenced disproportionately by one department or function. A lack of balance can lead to resentment, reduced collaboration, and ultimately, inefficiencies that affect the entire organization. How can you ensure that all functions have a voice and contribute equally to achieving your goals?

2. Reflect on whether your team members are aligned to a common purpose or if they are more focused on their individual or departmental interests. Misalignment can lead to conflicts, delays, and suboptimal outcomes. How can you communicate better and reinforce the organization's Main Thing to ensure that everyone is moving in the same direction?

3. Assess the extent to which leaders at all levels are transparent about the common objectives that everyone should be working toward.

4. Evaluate the nature of employee interactions. Do they seem more transactional or more collegial? Do employees gather on their own, or do you feel that you have to "manufacture" bonding?

5. Do project managers routinely tap into resources and manpower throughout the organization when they form their teams, or do cross-functional teams have to be forced?

6. Are there "bureaucratic barriers" to collaboration throughout the organization that you need to break down?

Turning Thought into Action

1. Consistently reinforce the organization's vision, mission, and strategic goals across all levels of the organization. Use various communication channels, from town halls to one-on-one meetings, to ensure that every employee understands the "main thing" and how their work contributes to it. By keeping the Main Thing front and center, you can ensure that collaboration efforts are aligned with the organization's overarching objectives.

2. Despite the benefits of remote work, face-to-face interactions remain crucial for building trust and fostering collaboration. Create opportunities for team members from different functions to come together in person to solve problems, brainstorm ideas, and make decisions. Whether through regular in-office days, off-site retreats, or project-based meetings, these interactions can strengthen relationships and improve collaborative outcomes.

3. Design your talent development programs to focus on the skills and behaviors essential for effective collaboration. This includes training in customer orientation, vision and strategy alignment, business acumen, accountability to execution, and the soft skills needed to work effectively with others. By aligning development efforts with the factors that drive collaboration, you can build a workforce that is equipped to work together towards common goals.

Resources

I have created a set of companion tools that can help you implement the concepts shared in the book. Here is a link to those tools:

Conclusion

Collaboration is a critical factor that can either propel your organization forward or hold it back. Poor collaboration, often rooted in a lack of trust, can have significant financial implications, manifesting in your financial statements as increased costs and inefficiencies. From inflated inventory levels to extended cash cycles, the hidden costs of poor collaboration can erode your bottom line in ways that are both subtle and substantial.

In this chapter, we have explored how collaboration—or the lack thereof—impacts not only the efficiency of your operations but also the financial health of your organization. We've examined the importance of trust, the challenges posed by remote and hybrid work environments, and the strategies that can help you foster a culture of collaboration that drives business success.

We demonstrated how Learning and Innovation and Trust and Collaboration are the key Factors in Fusion. Now, let's explore how these two factors intersect, the resulting dynamics that are created, and how they support a Momentum Culture.

COHERENCE & SAFETY

Fusion – Combining Learning & Innovation and Trust & Collaboration – Creating Coherence and Psychological Safety

Within Fusion, the cultural process that creates the energy for a Momentum Culture, are two critical Factors: Learning & Innovation and Trust & Collaboration. When those two Factors intersect, we create two critical Dynamics to a successful Momentum Culture, Psychological Safety and Coherence.

The connection between the two is straightforward. When you have an environment of Trust, and you combine that with a healthy approach to Risk, you create Psychological Safety. Psychological Safety is the bedrock upon which innovation stands. It is the assurance that employees can take risks, challenge ideas, and engage in healthy debate without fear of retribution. When employees feel safe to speak up and experiment, they unlock new possibilities for growth and adaptation, fueling the innovative spirit of the organization.

And when you foster a culture where what leaders say and do are consistent with what we invest our time to learn and our resources to invest in, we demonstrate Coherence. So, Coherence ensures that the organization's values are not just words but are lived and practiced consistently at every level. It is the alignment between what is said and what is done, creating a culture of trust and integrity. This alignment is crucial for building collaborative bonds that enable teams to work together effectively, driving collective success.

As we explore the role of Safety and Coherence in your organization, we'll see how these Dynamics create the fertile ground from which a Momentum Culture can emerge, empowering your teams to transform challenges into opportunities. These elements create a resilient, adaptable culture that can meet the demands of today's business environment with confidence and creativity.

PSYCHOLOGICAL SAFETY

Definition of Psychological Safety

Coined by Amy Edmondson, psychological safety encapsulates the environment where individuals feel secure in taking interpersonal risks—whether that means voicing concerns, sharing innovative ideas, or admitting mistakes—without the fear of negative repercussions. In this chapter, we'll explore how psychological safety acts as a catalyst in your Cultural Flywheel, turning potential energy into tangible business results by ensuring that every team member can contribute their best without fear.

Key Aspects of Psychological Safety

Psychological safety within Momentum Culture is built upon four foundational pillars: open communication, risk-taking, inclusivity, and a learning mindset. Open communication ensures that every team member, regardless of rank, has a voice that contributes to the organization's momentum, fostering stronger connections. Encouraging risk-taking allows employees to push boundaries and innovate. Inclusivity, a key element of Connection, ensures that diverse perspectives are integrated, creating a richer, more dynamic organizational culture. Finally, embracing mistakes as learning opportunities transforms setbacks into forward momentum, continuously propelling the Cultural Flywheel. Together, these elements not only sustain the energy within your organization but also amplify it, driving your business towards sustained success.

Importance in a Momentum Culture

When psychological safety is present, the Connection within teams strengthens, as trust and open dialogue remove barriers to collaboration. This interconnectedness accelerates the Innovation Capability of the organization, enabling faster innovation and more effective problem-solving. The impact is profound: employees become more engaged with each other, and more motivated to take on complex challenges, leading to higher performance and more consistent business outcomes.

Momentum Culture Assessment - Safety

In our assessment of psychological safety, we focus on understanding the extent to which employees feel secure in expressing differing opinions, challenging the status quo, and engaging in healthy conflict, even when it involves leadership. The assessment delves into how the organization fosters an environment where open dialogue is encouraged, where questioning and debating ideas—including those proposed by management—are seen as opportunities for growth rather than as threats. Additionally, we explore the organization's approach to risk-taking, assessing whether employees feel empowered to experiment and innovate without fear of negative consequences. By evaluating these aspects, the assessment aims to provide a comprehensive view of how psychological safety is nurtured within the organization, highlighting areas where trust and openness can be strengthened to support a more dynamic and resilient workplace culture.

BUILD YOUR CULTURAL FLYWHEEL

I. *Create Safe Opportunities for Feedback*

- Create a communication strategy that includes regular updates and opportunities for employees to ask questions, ensuring that everyone feels informed and included in the organization's direction.

- Train leaders to respond to feedback constructively, focusing on solutions rather than blame, to reinforce that the organization values openness and learning.

2. *Foster Transparent Communication*

- Establish regular communication channels where leadership transparently shares decisions, challenges, and upcoming changes with the entire organization.
- Encourage leaders to model transparency by being open about their own learning processes and mistakes, which can help build trust and reduce fear among employees.

3. *Promote Inclusive Decision-Making*

- Develop a structured process for decision-making that actively includes participation from multiple teams across the organization, ensuring that all perspectives are considered.
- Encourage leaders to seek out and value the perspectives of employees at all levels, recognizing that diverse viewpoints lead to more informed and effective decisions.

4. *Encourage Risk-Taking and Innovation*

- Celebrate failures as learning opportunities, sharing stories of risk-taking that lead to valuable insights, even if the initial attempt didn't succeed.
- Set clear expectations that innovation is a priority and reinforce this by recognizing and rewarding employees who take thoughtful risks, regardless of the outcome.

COHERENCE

Coherence within an organization refers to the alignment between what leaders say and what they do, and the consistency with which an organization's values are reflected in its practices and behaviors. It is the glue that binds the various elements of a company's culture, ensuring that the espoused values are not just words on a wall but are actively lived and experienced by everyone within the organization. When leaders embody the principles they promote, and when there is a strong alignment between the organization's stated values and everyday actions, coherence is achieved. This alignment is critical for building trust, engagement, and sustaining long-term success. In this section, we will delve into how coherence serves as the backbone of an effective organizational culture, reinforcing the trust and alignment that are essential for momentum.

Key Aspects of Coherence

Coherence in an organization can be understood through several key aspects: alignment of words and actions, consistency in decision-making, and accountability to shared values. First, the alignment of words and actions means that leaders must walk the talk; their behavior must reflect the values and commitments they communicate to their teams. Consistency in decision-making ensures that the principles guiding the organization are applied uniformly across all levels, avoiding the confusion and mistrust that arise from double standards. Lastly, accountability to shared values involves holding everyone in the organization, regardless of rank, responsible for living up to the organization's core values. This accountability reinforces a culture where integrity is valued, and everyone is committed to the same high standards, creating a cohesive and credible organizational environment.

Importance in a Momentum Culture

The importance of coherence in the workplace cannot be overstated. Research consistently shows that when there is a disconnect between what leaders say and what they do, employee trust erodes, leading to disengagement, reduced performance, and increased turnover. This was supported in our research, as the Coherence dynamic was the top driver of overall momentum. Moreover, research from Harvard Business Review showed that employees who perceive high levels of coherence between a company's stated values and leadership behavior are 5 times more likely to be engaged and 3 times more likely to stay with the organization long-term[14]. This alignment builds trust and credibility, which are essential for fostering a positive organizational culture. Moreover, coherence enhances decision-making, as consistent application of values and principles ensures that actions taken are in line with the organization's strategic goals, thereby driving better business outcomes. In the Momentum Culture framework, coherence is the invisible force that maintains the integrity of the Cultural Flywheel, ensuring that the energy generated by Connection and Capability is not lost but is instead directed towards sustained success.

Momentum Assessment - Coherence

In our assessment of organizational coherence, we focus on evaluating the alignment between leadership's words and actions, the consistency with which organizational values are upheld, and the degree to which accountability is maintained across all levels of the organization. We explore how well leaders model the behaviors and values they advocate for, ensuring that their actions reinforce the principles they communicate to the team. Additionally, the assessment examines how consistently these values are integrated into decision-making processes and whether there is a transparent and equitable approach to holding everyone accountable to these standards. By capturing insights into these dimensions, we aim to provide a clear picture of how coherence is experienced within the organization, identifying both strengths and areas for improvement in maintaining a culture of integrity and trust.

BUILD YOUR CULTURAL FLYWHEEL

I. *Align Words and Actions*
- Establish clear expectations for leaders to "walk the talk" by aligning their actions with the organization's stated values. Regularly review leadership decisions and behaviors to ensure they reflect the organization's commitments.

---

[14] (Groysberg, 2018)

- Encourage leaders to be transparent about the challenges they face in meeting commitments, fostering an environment of trust and mutual understanding.

2. *Enhance Accountability Across All Levels*

- Implement regular check-ins and performance reviews that emphasize accountability for living up to the organization's values. Ensure that these reviews are documented and followed up with actionable steps.

- Promote a culture of peer accountability by encouraging team members to hold each other to the organization's standards, fostering a collective sense of responsibility.

3. *Ensure Consistency in Decision-Making*

- Regularly audit decisions to check for consistency and fairness. Identify areas where decision-making may have deviated from the standard process.

- After decisions are made, clearly communicate the method that was used to make the decision, who made it, who contributed to it, and what criteria was used to drive the final path.

4. *Foster Transparency to Drive Coherence*

- Develop a transparent communication strategy that includes regular updates from leadership about decisions, changes, and the rationale behind them. This should be consistent across all levels of the organization.

- Create open forums or town halls where employees can ask questions and provide feedback directly to leadership, reinforcing the connection between transparency and trust.

Resources

I have created a set of companion tools that can help you implement the concepts shared in the book. Here is a link to those tools:

TURNING CHALLENGES INTO OPPORTUNITIES THROUGH FUSION

Throughout this section, we've explored how the elements of Learning and Innovation, and Trust and Collaboration form the bedrock of Fusion, enabling your organization to harness its collective energy and transform obstacles into catalysts for growth.

Learning and Innovation empower your workforce with the Capability to embrace risk, experiment fearlessly, and adapt to change with agility. Trust and Collaboration, however, are the connective tissues that bind your organization together. By bringing those factors together, you can create a culture that demonstrates Coherence which builds confidence that the organization will operate with integrity, matching action with its words. When this working environment also prioritizes Psychological Safety, mistakes become learning opportunities, and new ideas are welcomed as pathways to innovation. These Dynamics are hallmarks of a Momentum Culture.

But Fusion is just the beginning. While it provides the energy needed to drive your culture forward, that energy must be directed purposefully to achieve your strategic objectives. This is where the next element of the Momentum Culture framework comes into play: Vector. Just as Fusion fuels your organization with the power of Connection and Capability, Vector provides the direction for that energy, ensuring all efforts are aligned towards achieving your vision and strategic goals.

VECTOR

Physics vector - phys·ics vec·tor - /'fiziks 'vektər/

A quantity having both magnitude and direction, used to represent the position, velocity, or force in a physical system, ensuring that energy is directed with purpose towards a specific outcome.

Cultural vector - cul·tur·al vec·tor - /'kəlCH(ə)rəl 'vektər/

An organizational force that aligns the energy of a culture with its strategic goals and customer needs, ensuring that every effort is directed purposefully towards achieving meaningful and impactful results.

12
VECTOR

Vector in Motion – Directing Your Culture's Energy for Maximum Impact

Your culture is a force, but is it moving in the right direction? In the same way that a vector in mechanical physics has both magnitude and direction, your organization's cultural energy must be carefully aligned to achieve its full potential. This chapter explores the concept of Vector within the Momentum Culture framework—where the powerful energy generated by your people is channeled with purpose, ensuring that every action aligns with your strategic goals and drives customer-focused success.

Without a clear Vector, even the most vibrant culture can drift, expending energy without achieving the desired outcomes. Vector ensures that every effort is aligned with the organization's vision, strategy, and customer-centric goals, keeping your culture on course for success.

At the core of Vector lies two essential elements: Customer-Centricity and Vision and Strategic Alignment. Customer-Centricity focuses on ensuring that every aspect of your organization is aligned with the needs and expectations of your customers. It's about creating a culture where the customer's voice is heard at every level, and where success is measured by the value you deliver to those you serve.

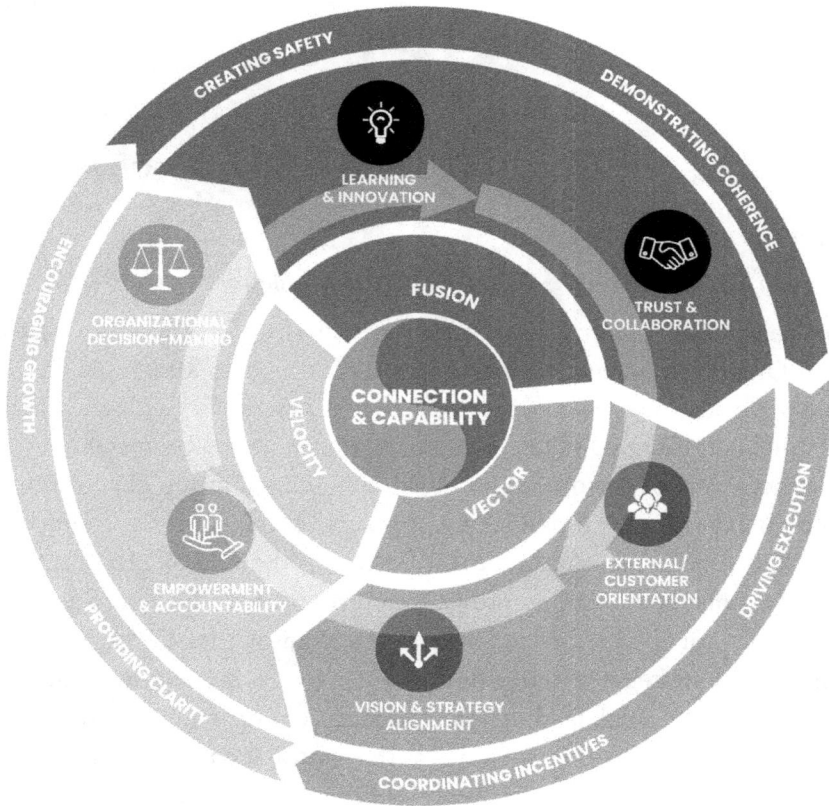

Vision and Strategic Alignment ensures that your organization's energy is consistently directed towards achieving your long-term goals, creating a cohesive strategy that drives the entire organization forward. As we delve deeper into these elements, we'll explore how Vector ensures that the cultural momentum you've built moves it in the right direction.

13
ALIGNMENT

Keeping the Main Thing, the Main Thing – the Criticality of Alignment

In the dynamic environment of business, clarity of purpose is a necessity. Organizations are not meant to be all things to all people. Quite the opposite, they are specific entities, comprised of a particular set of people, with focused talents, organized to generate unique value for a distinct group of customers, on behalf of a limited group of stakeholders. This focus is what defines a company's "Main Thing," the simplicity that helps it navigate the complexities of the market. To ensure it stays simple, leaders must provide their teams with a clear direction, ensuring that every effort and investment aligns with the organization's vision and strategy. Without this singular focus, the energy of an organization is wasted, leading to inefficiency, confusion, and ultimately, failure. Keeping the "Main Thing" as the central focus of all activities is not just about strategic alignment—it's about survival in a competitive world.

Things You Will Learn in This Chapter

• *The Power of Keeping the Main Thing, the Main Thing*: Learn why it's crucial for organizations to focus on their core mission and how straying from this focus can lead to entropy and decreased organizational effectiveness.

• *Understanding Entropy in Organizations:* Discover how the concept of entropy from physics applies to organizational alignment and how energy must be invested to maintain order and focus within a company.

- *The Role of Clear Communication in Alignment:* Explore how consistent and clear communication, including the use of memorable catchphrases or "memes," can help reinforce alignment to vision and strategy across all levels of the organization.

- *The Critical Link Between Alignment and Competitive Success:* Understand how aligning resources, strategies, and activities with your company's Main Thing is essential to maintain competitiveness, especially in times of resource constraints.

The Challenge of Alignment in Organizations

In physics, entropy is a measure of disorder or randomness in a system. It's a fundamental principle that systems naturally evolve toward a state of increased disorder unless energy is applied to maintain or restore order. This concept, though rooted in physics, has a profound metaphorical relevance to organizations. Just as physical systems require energy to combat entropy, organizations must exert continuous effort to maintain alignment with their vision and strategy. This is where alignment to vision and strategy becomes critical.

One of the most pervasive issues in organizations is the decline of alignment as you move down the hierarchy. While senior executives are typically confident in the company's vision and strategy, this clarity often diminishes as it filters through the ranks. The result is a disconnect where employees may not fully understand or believe in the direction the company is headed. This misalignment can lead to fragmented efforts, with different parts of the organization working at cross-purposes, rather than in a cohesive, synchronized manner.

This decline in alignment can be particularly frustrating for senior executives, who often see it as a straightforward challenge: communicate the vision and strategy, and the organization will follow. However, the reality is far more complex. Passive communication is not enough; active, consistent, and engaged efforts are required to truly align an organization. This includes not just talking about what needs to be done but investing time, resources, and energy into ensuring everyone in the organization understands, believes in, and is committed to the vision and strategy.

Failure to address these alignment issues doesn't just cause minor operational inefficiencies, it can lead to a disjointed culture and significant business failures. As resources become more constrained, the need for alignment intensifies. Companies must focus their scarce resources—whether that be time, money, or manpower—on the most critical initiatives. If they don't, they risk falling behind more disciplined competitors who are better aligned with their strategic goals.

The Struggle to Maintain Alignment

Alignment to vision and strategy is not just a top-down directive; it's a dynamic process that requires active management and continuous reinforcement throughout the organization. Unfortunately, alignment is one of the most challenging aspects for senior executives to sustain. As organizations grow in size and complexity, the natural tendency toward entropy increases, making it harder to keep everyone focused on the "main thing."

Passive alignment—where leaders assume that simply communicating the vision and strategy is sufficient—is rarely effective. Passive alignment often results in employees paying lip service to strategic goals without truly understanding or engaging with them. This superficial engagement can lead to a lack of commitment and accountability, which are essential for executing a successful strategy.

Active alignment, on the other hand, requires deliberate efforts to embed the vision and strategy into the daily activities and decision-making processes at all levels of the organization. This includes investing in training and development to enhance employees' business acumen, ensuring that they understand how their roles contribute to the overall strategy, and fostering a culture where alignment is continuously reinforced through consistent actions, communication, and resource allocation.

The complexity of maintaining alignment is further compounded by the reality that organizations are constantly evolving. Changes in market conditions, competitive pressures, and internal dynamics can all shift the strategic landscape, requiring ongoing adjustments to ensure that everyone remains aligned with the updated vision and goals. This continuous realignment is challenging, but it is essential to maintaining the organization's momentum and competitive edge.

In the absence of active alignment efforts, organizations risk drifting off course, with different departments or teams pursuing their own agendas rather than working in concert toward common objectives. This misalignment not only diminishes efficiency but can also lead to strategic failures, where the organization fails to capitalize on opportunities or mitigate risks effectively.

Research on the Impact of Alignment on Culture

The importance of alignment of culture to vision and strategy cannot be overstated. Organizations that master alignment tend to outperform their competitors, as their employees are more engaged, understand their roles more clearly, and work more cohesively towards common goals. Research by Deloitte[15] highlights that companies with a clear and unified vision experience 30% higher levels of innovation and 40% higher levels of retention compared to those without. Furthermore, these companies are 70% more likely to be top performers in their industry, underscoring the direct link between alignment and business success.

In our research, alignment emerged as a critical driver of employee perception of organizational competence and high performance. Employees who understand and believe in the organization's direction are more likely

---

[15] (Deloitte, 2016)

to bond with it, creating a sense of belonging and purpose. This alignment fosters a culture of commitment, where employees are not just working for a paycheck but are genuinely invested in the company's success.

Companies that excel in alignment do so because they have embedded it into their culture, ensuring that it is reflected in their values, practices, and daily operations. Transparency emerged as a key factor in fostering alignment. Organizations that effectively share progress towards goals and maintain open lines of communication tend to score higher on alignment metrics. Employees in these environments feel informed, trusted, and valued, which enhances their connection to the organization's vision. That feeling of confidence is significantly enhanced when the company invests in training around strategy and business acumen – so much so that it was the #1 Alignment element that predicted high cultural momentum.

However, one of the weakest areas of company performance identified in the research was the ability to minimize bureaucracy. Employees often perceive excessive bureaucracy as a sign of misalignment, where the organization's structures and processes are not effectively supporting its core business objectives. This perception of inefficiency can erode trust and engagement, leading to a disconnect between employees and the company's strategic goals.

> *"Eliminate unnecessary systems and bureaucracy that bloat strategy and processes."*
>
> —Research Responses

Culture Accelerators consistently highlighted the effectiveness of communication in their organizations. They appreciated the clear line of sight between their individual goals and the overall strategy, and they felt confident that they could articulate the company's strategy if asked.

"Aligning all departmental goals and KPIs directly with the company's overarching vision and strategy would likely have the most positive impact on business performance."

—Research Responses

In contrast, Culture Decelerators often cited a lack of consistency in communication as a key issue. While they generally had a positive view of the organization, they felt that there was room for improvement in how alignment was maintained and reinforced. These employees often asked for more communication, particularly in the form of consistent updates and clarity around strategic priorities.

One of the most surprising findings from the research was the significant impact of business acumen and strategy training on alignment. The primary driver of confidence in alignment to vision and strategy was not just communication but the organization's investment in developing employees' understanding of business fundamentals. Employees who received training in areas such as market dynamics, competition, and value creation were far more likely to feel aligned with the organization's strategy. This suggests that alignment is not just about telling people what the strategy is but also about equipping them with the knowledge and skills they need to contribute to its execution effectively.

Organizations that fail to invest in these areas often struggle with alignment. Employees in these environments frequently commented on the lack of meaningful training opportunities, which left them feeling disconnected from the overall market context and uncertain about how their work contributed to the organization's success. This gap in understanding can lead to a fragmented organization, where different departments or teams pursue their own agendas rather than working together towards a common goal.

In summary, alignment is a multifaceted challenge that requires more than just clear communication from leadership. It involves a deep integration of the organization's vision and strategy into its culture, processes, and training programs. By fostering a culture of transparency, minimizing bureaucracy, and investing in business acumen development, organizations can significantly enhance their alignment and, in turn, their overall performance.

CASE EXAMPLE: AT&T

Problem

To illustrate the impact of alignment on organizational success, consider the 2007 case of the newly formed AT&T, then the largest telecom in the world, which faced an enormous challenge in the wake of consolidating several US regional telephone companies. The newly formed behemoth, then with over $265 billion in assets, was transitioning from a traditional public utility to a cutting-edge telecom services company. This shift was not merely about integrating assets; it was about redefining the culture and operational strategy of a massive workforce accustomed to a utility mindset—focused on safety, cost control, and low innovation.

The stakes were incredibly high. Approximately $135 billion of the company's assets were classified as goodwill from acquisitions, and with a weighted average cost of capital (WACC) of about 6%, the company needed to generate roughly $8 billion annually just to cover this intangible asset's cost. The risk of failure was enormous, leading to a massive write-down on the balance sheet, a sharp decline in stock value, and billions in lost shareholder value.

Company leadership recognized that aligning the culture with the new strategic direction was critical to success. They needed to transition from a low-risk, low-innovation mindset to one that embraced collaboration, technological advancement, and a customer-centric approach. This required not just a change in strategy but a deep cultural transformation.

Solution

The CEO understood that half-measures would not suffice. He engaged my former consulting firm to design and implement a comprehensive leadership development and strategy alignment program aimed at cascading through three levels of leadership, covering 6,500 leaders across the organization[16].

The solution included a business simulation that allowed leaders to experience firsthand what it would take to deliver shareholder value in this new company. The simulation focused on understanding the culture change required, drawing on John Kotter's principles of leading change, and emphasized the financial foundations of return on invested capital (ROIC) and how to grow shareholder value.

In addition to the simulation, the team and I helped the company characterize the culture necessary for success in its new business model. They identified the delta between the current culture—rooted in the old utility model—and the desired culture of an innovative, high-tech telecommunications company. This clarity around the needed culture shift was instrumental in aligning leadership and, ultimately, the entire organization.

Outcomes

The impact of the alignment initiative was profound. From 2008 to 2012, AT&T stock value doubled, a clear indication of the market's confidence in the company's new direction. Remarkably, over half of its revenue in 2012 came from products and services that didn't exist before the merger, demonstrating the success of their innovation and cultural shift.

Moreover, the company managed to avoid the need for a massive goodwill write-down, preserving billions in shareholder value. The cultural transformation enabled it to pivot effectively and become a competitive player in the fast-evolving telecom landscape.

---

[16] BTS

This case exemplifies the critical role that alignment to vision and strategy plays in driving business success. By aligning their leadership and workforce around a clear strategic direction and the necessary cultural shifts, this new technology company was able to achieve its ambitious goals and create significant shareholder value.

LEVERAGE POINTS:

- Real alignment requires getting people's attention. Small moves are not going to do that, so be bold,
- You will not be successful with new business models with old ways of thinking and working. You need to start from the ground up. Ask yourself, "If we were going to be the best in the world at this new business, what would everyone need to thinking, saying and doing, that is different than today?"

MAKING THE SHIFT TO A MOMENTUM CULTURE OF ALIGNMENT

For the Organization

In a Momentum Culture, the organization ensures that all efforts align with its core mission and vision. This involves strategic goal setting, leadership alignment, and integrated performance management. Leadership workshops and cross-departmental planning are essential to maintain unity in purpose and strategic focus. The organization values strategic thinking, market responsiveness, and customer-centricity, perceiving employees as integral to driving its mission. Structures like performance dashboards and coaching programs ensure that all actions reflect the broader vision, fostering a culture of accountability and coherence.

For Individuals

Individuals in a Momentum Culture align their actions with the organization's vision, prioritizing tasks that contribute to strategic goals. They demonstrate adaptability to strategic shifts and balance short-term needs with long-term objectives. Strategic planning, analytical thinking, and financial acumen are key skills, supported by a mindset focused on long-term success, purpose-driven work, and systems-thinking. Employees feel empowered to align their work with the organization's purpose, knowing their contributions drive collective success and sustainable growth.

MOMENTUM CULTURE MODEL FOR ALIGNMENT

	Individuals	Organizations
	Behaviors	**Processes & Capabilities**
Extrinsic	• **Prioritizes Time and Resources:** Consistently allocates time and resources to activities that align with the organization's strategic goals. • **Adapts to Strategic Shifts:** Quickly adjusts efforts and approaches in response to changes in the organization's strategy. • **Balances Short-Term and Long-Term Goals:** Effectively manages the tension between immediate needs and long-term objectives, ensuring both are adequately addressed.	• **Effective Resource Allocation:** Systematically allocates resources (financial, human, and technological) in a way that aligns with strategic priorities and long-term objectives. • **Strategic Goal Setting:** Sets clear, measurable, and achievable goals that align with the broader vision and strategy, ensuring all efforts are focused on the right outcomes. • **Leadership Strategic Alignment:** Consistently trains and coaches leaders to understand, communicate, and model the organization's strategic vision, ensuring their teams are aligned. • **Integrated Performance Management:** Integrates performance management systems with strategic goals, ensuring that individual and team performance directly supports the organization's vision.

Skills

- **Strategic Planning:** Skill in setting and executing plans that align with the organization's long-term vision.
- **Analytical Thinking:** The ability to analyze complex information and make decisions that align with strategic priorities.
- **Financial Acumen:** Understanding of financial principles and the impact of strategic decisions on the organization's financial health.

Structures & Resources

- **Leadership Alignment Workshops:** Conducts regular workshops that bring leaders together to discuss, refine, and align their understanding of the organization's strategic vision.
- **Integrated Performance Dashboards:** Creates dashboards that link performance metrics directly to strategic goals, allowing leaders to monitor progress and adjust as needed.
- **Performance Review Systems:** Uses systems that integrate strategic goals into employee performance reviews, ensuring that individual efforts contribute to the broader organizational vision.
- **Leadership Coaching Programs:** Provides ongoing coaching for leaders focused on aligning their decisions and behaviors with the organization's strategic goals.
- **Cross-Departmental Planning Sessions:** Conducts regular cross-departmental collaboration sessions on aligning their initiatives with the organization's strategic goals.

Mindsets

- **Long-Term Focus:** I believe that maintaining a long-term perspective is essential for sustained success, and I approach the world with a focus on future outcomes.
- **Purpose-Driven:** I believe that understanding and aligning with the organization's core mission is key to meaningful work, and I approach the world with a commitment to purpose.
- **Systems-Thinking:** I believe that understanding how all parts of the organization fit together is key to effective decision-making, and I approach the world with a focus on the interconnections within the system.

Values

- **Purpose-Driven:** We believe that understanding and aligning with the organization's core mission is key to meaningful work, and we are committed to purpose-driven actions.
- **Strategic Thinking:** We believe that strategic thinking should guide all decisions, ensuring that every action contributes to our broader vision.
- **Market Responsiveness:** We believe in staying attuned to market trends and customer needs, ensuring that our strategy remains relevant and competitive.
- **Customer-Centricity:** We prioritize aligning our strategic goals with the needs and expectations of our customers, ensuring they are at the heart of our decisions.

Intrinsic

Perception

"I believe I am part of an organization that is committed to its long-term vision and strategic goals. In this environment, my work is aligned with a clear purpose, and I am encouraged to think strategically and adapt to changes in the market. I feel empowered to prioritize my time and resources effectively, knowing that my efforts contribute to both immediate needs and long-term objectives. Together, we create an organization that is focused, agile, and responsive to the evolving needs of our customers and the market."

"We see our employees as deeply aligned with our core mission, driven by a clear sense of purpose in their work. They consistently apply strategic thinking to their decisions, ensuring that every action they take contributes to our broader vision. Our employees are attuned to market trends and customer needs, proactively adapting their efforts to maintain our competitive edge and meet the evolving expectations of our customers. Their commitment to purpose-driven actions, strategic thinking, and responsiveness to external factors ensures that our organization remains focused, agile, and aligned with both our internal goals and the dynamic environment in which we operate."

BUILDING YOUR CULTURAL FLYWHEEL

To build a cultural flywheel that aligns with your vision and strategy, you must ensure that every part of your organization is moving cohesively in the same direction. This requires consistent effort, strategic focus, and a commitment to both intrinsic and extrinsic factors.

Thought-Provoking Questions:

- If asked, do you believe most employees would articulate the organization's "Main Thing" in a way that aligns with your expectations?

- What is your company's execution fundamental that creates value within your organization? How well do your teams connect their activities toward this core process?

- How well do your employees understand why the company exists, how it makes money, and how their work contributes to these goals?

- Do your meetings and gatherings overtly focus on aligning people to your vision and strategy? Are you intentional about connecting these dots?

Turning Thought into Action:

- Constantly reinforce the key messages that define your vision and strategy. Utilize every communication channel to ensure that these messages are heard, understood, and acted upon across the organization.

- Create opportunities for employees to learn about the business, develop their financial fluency, and understand how their roles contribute to the organization's success. Use these moments to align teams around your strategic goals.

- Ensure that all talent development initiatives are aligned with the core issues that drive collaboration and success in your organization. Focus on customer orientation, vision and strategy alignment, business acumen, accountability, and the soft skills needed to execute these strategies effectively.

- By focusing on these areas, you can create a powerful cultural flywheel that keeps your organization aligned with its vision and strategy, driving sustained success and competitive advantage.

Resources

I have created a set of companion tools that can help you implement the concepts shared in the book. Here is a link to those tools:

Conclusion

When everyone in the company is pulling in the same direction, focusing on the "main thing," you create a powerful momentum that drives sustainable performance. The key to this alignment is not only in setting clear goals, but in communicating them relentlessly, embedding them into the culture, and ensuring that every decision and action reflects that focus.

By keeping the "Main Thing" at the forefront, you enable your organization to navigate complexities and resist the pull of entropy. This clarity not only simplifies decision-making but also empowers employees to contribute meaningfully to the company's goals, fostering a culture where everyone is aligned with the overarching strategy.

The consequences of misalignment are stark—wasted resources, diluted efforts, and missed opportunities. But when alignment is achieved, it acts as a force multiplier, turning vision into reality, and strategy into action. This chapter illustrates how alignment can transform an organization, ensuring that every person, process, and project is driving towards the same end.

As we conclude this chapter on alignment, it's essential to recognize that alignment doesn't stop at the internal workings of your company. It extends outward, influencing how you interact with and serve your customers. After all, the most aligned organizations are those that place the customer at the heart of their strategy. In the next chapter, we'll explore how a customer-centric orientation can serve as the Main Thing for your business, driving growth, innovation, and loyalty in ways that mere alignment to strategy cannot achieve alone.

14

CUSTOMER CENTRICITY

Who is the Hero in Your Story? Keeping Customers at the Center of Your Culture

In every great story, the hero takes center stage. In the story of Momentum Cultures, that hero is the customer. Unfortunately, in many companies, the hero gets lost amid competing priorities, internal processes, and operational complexities. As organizations grow, they often become more inwardly focused, prioritizing efficiency and profitability over customer needs. However, in a truly customer-centric culture, the customer is the "Main Thing" —the guiding force that shapes decisions, strategies, and daily actions. Without this alignment, the story falters, and the organization drifts away from its purpose. This chapter will explore what it means to keep the customer as the hero of your story and how this focus drives business success and cultural momentum.

Things You Will Learn in This Chapter:

- *Understanding Your Customer Orientation:* Assess whether your organization is internally driven, customer-aware, customer-focused, or customer-obsessed. This understanding is key to driving customer success and ensuring that the customer is at the heart of your operations.

- *Organizational Structure Aligned with Customer Needs:* Analyze whether your company's structure supports your customers' buying process or merely serves internal needs. A true customer-centric organization aligns its processes with customer success.

- *Gathering and Operationalizing Customer Insights:* Discover how to establish processes for gathering, analyzing, and applying customer feedback to continuously improve products, services, and customer experiences.

- *Rewards and Recognition for Customer Success:* Learn how to align employee rewards and recognition programs with customer success metrics to foster a culture where everyone contributes to delivering exceptional customer experiences.

Understanding the Natural Drift Away from Customer-Centricity

Over time, as companies grow and mature, there's an inevitable drift away from customer-centricity. This drift isn't intentional; it's a result of several factors that naturally push organizations toward internal focus and away from their customers. This is especially true in matrixed organizations, where functions become specialized and can lose sight of how they contribute to customer value. The internal focus can lead to a situation where the customer becomes abstracted, making it harder for employees to see how their work impacts customer success.

The Meeting Culture Trap

A poignant example of this slide into internal focus is from when I was at Metrowerks, a software company that was acquired by Motorola. Metrowerks was initially highly customer-centric, with customers that acted more like "fans" than just people who bought products from us. But after we were absorbed into Motorola, the culture shifted towards an internal focus, marked by an explosion of meetings. The increase in meetings—many of which lacked clear connections to customer needs—began to erode the company's product development speed and quality. Recognizing the problem, the CEO mandated that any meeting must be justified by how it served customer needs, allowing employees to leave any meeting that didn't clearly meet this expectation after the first five minutes. This initiative was ingenious in that it was simple and cost-free, yet instantly forced the organization to refocus on its customers.

> *"If the meeting organizer cannot convincingly articulate how that meeting benefits a customer in some way, you have my expressed permission to get up and leave."*

—Research Responses

The Rising Tide of Customer Expectations and Competitive Pressures

In today's rapidly evolving business environment, customer expectations are continuously rising, driven by what is often referred to as the "Amazon effect." This phenomenon describes how companies like Amazon have set a new standard for customer service, particularly in areas like speed, personalization, and convenience. These elevated expectations don't just apply to consumer goods but are influencing B2B relationships as well. Customers now expect the same level of efficiency, customization, and proactive service from all their suppliers, regardless of industry.

At the same time, competition is intensifying across sectors. Barriers to entry are lowering, allowing new, agile competitors to disrupt established markets more easily. These new entrants often employ innovative business models that focus intensely on customer needs, putting additional pressure on traditional companies to adapt quickly or risk becoming irrelevant.

This dual challenge—rising customer expectations and increasing competition—makes customer-centricity more critical than ever. However, maintaining a strong customer focus is challenging, especially in large, complex organizations where internal processes and priorities can obscure the customer's voice.

RESEARCH ON THE IMPACT OF CUSTOMER CENTRICITY ON CULTURE

Our research highlighted the criticality of employees' relationship with customers. When employees feel closely connected to customers, cultures are stronger. And one of the strongest predictors of high momentum cultures is a feeling of love – that customers "love us", and that customer relationships are more than transactional.

A Key Disconnect Between Beliefs and Actions

The research revealed a significant disconnect in many organizations between their self-perception as being customer-focused and the reality of how they operate. This discrepancy is striking, especially when employees score their companies highly on being customer-centric in surveys but simultaneously give low marks on whether the company incentivizes actions that truly benefit customers. This gap highlights a critical issue: while many organizations believe they are putting the customer first, their structures, incentives, and daily operations often tell a different story.

A Unified Customer Perspective Across All Functions

The most significant driver of a customer-centric culture, as our research indicates, is whether employees perceive that a unified and pervasive picture of the customer permeates across all functions within the company. When all departments, from marketing and sales to product development and customer service, share a consistent and holistic view of the customer, it becomes much easier to align actions and strategies with customer needs. This alignment fosters a culture where every decision is made with the customer in mind, leading to better products, services, and ultimately, stronger business results.

A Desire for Deeper Customer Connections

Cultural Accelerators express a strong desire to deepen connections with customers. They often advocate for more opportunities to interface directly with customers, rather than relying on a revolving door of less experienced employees in customer-facing roles. Accelerators also call for more comprehensive training on customer needs, businesses, and strategies, as they believe this knowledge is crucial for serving customers effectively. Moreover, they push for more frequent and meaningful feedback from customers, which they see as essential for continuous improvement and innovation.

> *"Arrange time for employees to get to interact with our customers directly to understand their need better."*
>
> —Research Responses

Feeling Underequipped and Overwhelmed

On the other hand, cultural Decelerators often feel they lack the resources necessary to serve customers effectively. They frequently mention that the organization is trying to do too much, leading to situations where customer experience suffers. These employees often feel overwhelmed, believing that the front line is being set up for failure because the company is stretching itself too thin, unable to meet customer expectations consistently.

> *"Stop over-promising to the customer, and under-resourcing the support team."*
>
> —Research Responses

KEY INSIGHTS

Structures and Processes Matter

A critical insight is the importance of having structures and processes that genuinely serve the customer. If a customer were to design your company's processes, would they look the same as they do now? Are your products and services structured to support the customer's buying process, or are they optimized for your sales process? These questions are essential for ensuring that the organization is truly customer focused.

Everyone Needs to Know Their Role

Every employee should be able to draw a clear, direct line from what they do to how it impacts the customer. This clarity is part of keeping the main thing, the main thing. When employees understand how their work contributes to customer success, they are more engaged and aligned with the organization's goals.

Simple Metrics for Success

To measure whether customer relationships are improving or deteriorating, it's crucial to have clear, simple metrics like Net Promoter Score (NPS) or Customer Loyalty metrics like churn. These metrics should be widely reported, frequently referenced, and linked to employee bonuses to ensure that everyone is focused on customer success.

CASE EXAMPLE: MOTOROLA SEMICONDUCTOR/FREESCALE

Addressing a Growing Disconnect Between Company and Customer

At Motorola Semiconductor, later rebranded as Freescale, the company faced significant challenges as its financial performance began to decline, and it started losing key design contracts that it historically would have secured. The company's core strengths—quality, speed, and delivery—began to erode, which alarmed both internal stakeholders and long-standing customers.

The root of the problem lay in the company's inward focus. Over time, the organization became increasingly insular, relying on its past reputation as a market leader and failing to engage meaningfully with its customers. This detachment led to a growing cultural sickness, where the company's leadership was not fully aware of how far they had strayed from meeting their customers' evolving needs. The issue was perceived by customers as arrogance—a belief that Motorola knew better than the market about what was needed.

Installing a Customer Loyalty Function and Reorienting Culture

To combat these issues, the company established a dedicated Customer Loyalty function, tasked with acting as a listening post and spearheading efforts to gather and analyze customer feedback. My team was responsible for proactively engaging with customers through one-on-one contacts, comprehensive surveys, and the establishment of a simple customer health metric, designed to assess the health of customer relationships and identify systemic issues impacting customer loyalty.

A key initiative was the development of a "Customer Loyalty Bootcamp," an interactive experience where executives participated in a simulation that allowed them to step into their customers' shoes. By viewing the company from the customer's perspective, leaders could better understand the frustration and dissatisfaction that customers were experiencing. This program began with the CEO and his direct reports, eventually cascading down through the director level at Freescale.

Additionally, customer loyalty metrics were integrated into the executive pay plan. This ensured customer satisfaction data was gathered and acted on at the highest levels of the organization. Regular quarterly pulse surveys provided ongoing insights, and the Customer Loyalty director was given the responsibility to report on these metrics at quarterly operations meetings.

Finally, the company created a structured process for analyzing customer data and developing actionable solutions, which were then shared with customers. Customer Loyalty Core Teams were formed within each function and business unit to unpack survey results and feedback, ensuring that every part of the organization was aligned and responsive to customer needs.

Rebuilding Trust and Reclaiming Market Leadership

The journey was not without its challenges. In the second survey cycle, customer loyalty scores dipped as customers initially reacted to the changes. However, as the company continued its efforts, these scores began to rise steadily. Customers started to notice the genuine changes and improvements in the company's approach, leading to a restoration of trust and satisfaction.

One significant milestone was with an automotive customer who had previously given Freescale its worst supplier grade. Within three years, this customer ranked Freescale as their top supplier, a testament to the effectiveness of the company's cultural and operational transformation.

Overall, customer loyalty scores improved consistently over three years, correlating with successive years of better customer retention and gross margin performance. This positive momentum ultimately contributed to Freescale's successful acquisition and merger with NXP, a move that was partly fueled by the company's renewed customer-centric focus.

LEVERAGE POINTS

- Listening to the Customer. Investments like establishing a Customer Loyalty function or integrating customer feedback into core business processes help the company reorient its culture around customer needs. Momentum Cultures pivot around the customer, not the other way around.

- Accountability Drives Behavior. Tying customer satisfaction metrics to executive compensation ensured that customer-centricity was prioritized at the highest levels. The old saying is "behavior follows compensation". If you want employees - executives down to the front line - to make decisions on behalf of the customer, make sure they are incentivized to do so.

- Experiences Change Mindset. Experiences like the Customer Loyalty Bootcamp provide executives with transformative perspectives, helping them understand and empathize with customers, which was crucial for driving cultural change. Mindsets are formed by experience, so if you want leaders to adopt a new mindset, you must give them new experiences. And those experiences must be powerful, utilizing emotion as much as facts.

MAKING THE SHIFT TO A MOMENTUM CULTURE OF CUSTOMER CENTRICITY

For Organizations:

To shift towards a Momentum Culture of Customer Centricity, organizations must embed customer-focused processes and capabilities at every level. This involves systematically integrating customer feedback into decision-making, ensuring cross-functional teams collaborate on customer solutions, and utilizing tools like Customer Success Dashboards to track and enhance customer satisfaction. By aligning organizational structures and resources with customer-centric values, the organization fosters an environment where long-term customer relationships and continuous improvement drive sustainable success.

For Individuals:

Individuals making the shift to a Momentum Culture of Customer Centricity should adopt a customer-first mentality, actively seeking feedback and advocating for the customer's needs in every decision. By focusing on continuous improvement and collaborating cross-functionally, employees ensure that their actions are aligned with customer success. Developing skills in customer insight analysis and data-driven decision-making will empower individuals to contribute meaningfully to the organization's customer-centric goals, ultimately enhancing the overall customer experience.

MOMENTUM CULTURE MODEL FOR CUSTOMER CENTRICITY

	Individuals	Organizations
	Behaviors	**Processes & Capabilities**
Extrinsic	• **Seeks Customer Feedback:** Regularly gathers and uses customer feedback to improve products, services, and the overall customer experience. • **Aligns Processes with Customer Success:** Ensures that all processes and workflows are designed to support and enhance customer success. • **Advocates for the Customer:** Acts as a voice for the customer within the organization, ensuring that their needs and expectations are considered in decision-making. • **Collaborates Cross-Functionally:** Works effectively with colleagues across departments to create solutions that meet customer needs holistically.	• **Customer Insight Integration:** Systematically integrates customer feedback and insights into decision-making processes across the organization. • **Cross-Functional Collaboration on Customer Solutions:** Brings together diverse teams from across the organization to collaborate on solutions that address customer needs holistically. • **Customer Success Measurement:** Develops, tracks, and acts on customer success metrics to drive continuous improvement in customer satisfaction. • **Holistic Customer Experience Management:** Manages the entire customer experience across all touchpoints, ensuring consistency and alignment with the organization's customer-centric goals.
	Skills	**Structures & Resources**
Intrinsic	• **Customer Insight Analysis:** Analyzes customer data and feedback to derive meaningful insights that drive improvements. • **Communication:** Skilled in clearly and effectively conveying information and ideas to customers and colleagues. • **Data-Driven Decision-Making:** Uses data to inform decisions, particularly those that impact the customer experience.	• **Cross-Functional Collaboration Tools:** Deploys software that enables seamless collaboration across departments, facilitating the development of customer-focused solutions. • **Customer Success Dashboards:** Uses visual dashboards that track and display key customer success metrics, allowing teams to monitor performance and make data-driven decisions. • **Voice of the Customer (VoC) Integration Tools:** Creates systems that integrate customer feedback into every stage of the product or service lifecycle, ensuring their voice is central to decision-making.

Mindsets	Values
• **Customer-First Mentality:** I believe that the customer's needs should always come first, and I approach the world with a focus on delivering value to them. • **Continuous Improvement:** I believe that there is always room to enhance the customer experience, and I approach the world with a focus on constant growth and improvement.	• **Commitment to Excellence:** We are dedicated to striving for the highest standards in customer service and satisfaction, continuously seeking ways to improve. • **Customer-Centric Innovation:** We innovate with a focus on creating products, services, and experiences that align with and exceed customer expectations. • **Long-Term Customer Relationships:** We prioritize building lasting relationships with our customers, understanding that long-term success depends on their satisfaction and loyalty.

Perception

"I believe that the customer's needs should always come first. I am committed to delivering value by constantly improving the customer experience and ensuring that my work is aligned with their success. I collaborate across departments to advocate for the customer, using data-driven insights to inform decisions that enhance their overall experience."	"We believe in a commitment to excellence and innovation focused on the customer. We prioritize building long-term relationships by integrating customer feedback into our processes, fostering cross-functional collaboration, and continuously improving our services to exceed customer expectations and ensure their satisfaction and loyalty."

BUILDING YOUR CULTURAL FLYWHEEL

Creating a momentum culture that truly centers on customer orientation requires intentional and sustained effort. To build this cultural flywheel, ensure that every part of your organization is aligned and moving in the same direction, consistently working towards a customer-centric approach.

Here are some thought-provoking questions and actionable steps to help you build momentum in your customer-centric culture:

Thought-Provoking Questions:

1. How often do you remind your employees that the customer is the hero in your story? Does every employee understand the customer's role in the success of your business?

2. Consider the current organizational structure: Does it serve your internal processes more than your customers? How might a customer restructure your company to better serve their needs?

3. How visible are your customers' needs and feedback within your company? Do employees regularly reference customer insights when making decisions?

4. Would you buy from your own company? Have you thoroughly examined the customer 's journey to ensure it's as smooth and satisfying as possible?

Turning Thought into Action:

1. Encourage a mindset where employees in every function see themselves as part of the customer service team, regardless of their role and understand how their work impacts the customer experience. Equip your teams with the skills needed to creatively solve customer problems.

2. Make customer feedback a fundamental part of your operational processes. This could mean regular pulse checks with customers and ensuring their feedback directly informs product development and service improvements.

3. Align rewards and recognition systems at all levels with customer success metrics.

4. Focus your key communications on customer-centricity. Ensure leaders consistently convey the importance of the customer in every communication, making these messages viral within the organization.

By focusing on these elements, you can create a self-sustaining culture that continually propels your organization forward, always keeping the customer at the heart of everything you do.

Resources

I have created a set of companion tools that can help you implement the concepts shared in the book. Here is a link to those tools:

Conclusion

By making the customer the hero, you've aligned your organization to a purpose that transcends internal processes and structures. You've begun to embed customer-centric values, skills, and behaviors across every level, ensuring that your culture reflects the brand promise you make to your customers. When everyone in the company is focused on helping the hero succeed, the entire organization moves with a unified, unstoppable force.

But the story doesn't end here. To maintain this momentum and ensure that customer-centricity is more than just a fleeting focus, it must be interwoven with your company's vision and strategy. This is where the concept of Vector comes into play—the combination of Alignment to Vision and Strategy with Customer Centricity. It's not enough to just serve your customers well; you must ensure that every action taken is aligned with your overarching goals and strategic direction.

In the next chapter, we'll delve into how this powerful combination of alignment and customer orientation creates a Vector that propels your organization forward, ensuring that every effort contributes to sustainable growth and success.

15

COORDINATING INCENTIVES & DRIVING EXECUTION

The Intersection of Customer Centricity and Alignment to Strategy – Steering the Momentum of Vector

At the core of Vector, the cultural construct that provides direction and focus within your organization, lie two essential Factors: Customer Centricity and Alignment to Vision and Strategy. When these two Factors intersect, they drive cultures to be more externally focused, and for all employees to support that focus with their daily work. That direction is created by two critical Dynamics in a Momentum Culture: Coordinating Incentives and Driving Execution.

Coordinating Incentives ensures that every employee's goals and rewards are intricately connected to the company's overarching vision and strategic priorities. This alignment is not just about motivating individual performance; it's about creating a unified force where every effort is directed toward common objectives, fostering a culture of shared purpose and commitment. When incentives are strategically aligned, all members of the organization are motivated to move in harmony towards the same goals, amplifying the impact of each contribution.

Driving Execution is the mechanism that transforms strategic intent into action. It involves structuring the organization around customer interactions, ensuring that the focus remains outward-looking, and that execution is driven by customer needs rather than internal processes. Moreover, it emphasizes the development of leaders who possess the acumen and strategic insight to navigate challenges and drive the organization forward with minimal bureaucratic friction. Effective execution turns plans into results, ensuring that the organization's momentum is not just maintained but accelerated.

As we delve into the role of Coordinating Incentives and Driving Execution in your organization, we'll explore how these elements create a vector, steering the momentum of your culture, ensuring that your energy is channeled efficiently towards achieving your strategic goals.

COORDINATING INCENTIVES

Coordinating Incentives is the organizational practice of ensuring that employee rewards, recognition, and performance metrics are directly tied to the company's strategic objectives and customer success. This alignment helps every employee understand how their individual contributions link to broader organizational goals, thereby motivating them to act in ways that propel the company toward its strategic vision.

Key Aspects of Coordinating Incentives

Coordinating incentives within a Momentum Culture involves several critical elements: connecting employee goals to the company's vision and strategic direction, tying incentives to tangible business outcomes, and prioritizing customer-centric rewards. First, employees must see a clear connection between their work and the company's broader mission, which engages them and motivates them to perform at their best. Second, incentives should be linked to measurable business outcomes like revenue growth and customer satisfaction, ensuring that performance directly contributes to the organization's success. Finally, customer-centric rewards emphasize improving customer satisfaction and loyalty, ensuring that employee efforts align with the company's commitment to delivering exceptional value to its customers.

Importance in a Momentum Culture

Coordinating incentives is crucial in a Momentum Culture as it fosters a culture of accountability, focus, and high performance. When employees understand how their roles and rewards are connected to the company's strategic goals, they are more likely to be engaged and productive. Research from Willis Towers Watson reveals that companies with well-aligned incentives experience a 30% increase in employee engagement and a 20% boost in performance outcomes. Moreover, coordinating incentives with customer success has a profound impact on business results, leading to significantly higher customer retention rates and revenue growth. By ensuring that incentives are aligned with both internal goals and customer value, organizations can drive sustained success and long-term growth.

Momentum Culture Assessment - Coordinating Incentives

In assessing the alignment of incentives within an organization, we focus on how well employee incentives are tied to customer success metrics, whether rewards are focused on tangible business outcomes, and if employee goals are clearly connected to the company's vision and strategy. The assessment explores the degree to which incentives are designed to drive the organization's strategic objectives and whether these incentives effectively motivate employees to deliver value to customers. By evaluating these aspects, the assessment aims to provide a comprehensive understanding of how well incentives are aligned with both the company's internal goals and its commitment to customer success.

BUILD YOUR CULTURAL FLYWHEEL

I. *Communicate Strategic Objectives Clearly*

- Ensure that the company's vision and strategy are communicated effectively to all employees. This clarity helps employees understand how their individual goals align with the broader organizational direction.

- Regularly review and update communication strategies to ensure that every employee remains aligned with the company's evolving goals.

2. *Link Performance Metrics to Strategic Goals*

   - Design performance metrics that are directly tied to the company's strategic priorities. This ensures that employees are rewarded for activities that drive the organization towards its goals.

   - Implement continuous feedback loops to adjust performance metrics as business priorities shift, maintaining alignment with strategic objectives.

3. *Incentivize Customer Success*

   - Develop incentives that reward employees for achieving customer success metrics, such as satisfaction, retention, and loyalty. This alignment ensures that employee behavior supports the company's commitment to delivering exceptional customer value.

   - Incorporate customer feedback into the incentive structure to keep employees focused on what matters most to customers.

4. *Monitor and Adjust Incentive Programs*

   - Regularly assess the effectiveness of incentive programs to ensure they remain aligned with evolving business strategies and customer needs.

   - Make data-driven adjustments to incentives based on performance outcomes, ensuring that they continue to motivate desired behaviors and drive business success.

   - By focusing on these practices, organizations can create a culture where incentives are not only aligned with strategic goals but also drive the behaviors needed to achieve long-term success.

DRIVING EXECUTION

Driving execution refers to an organization's capability to effectively turn strategies into actions and achieve its objectives. It involves the coordination of people, processes, and resources to ensure that strategic goals are met efficiently. Execution is about translating plans into measurable outcomes, ensuring that every part of the organization is aligned and working toward common goals.

Key Aspects of Driving Execution

Driving execution within a Momentum Culture is built on five key pillars: clear communication of objectives, accountability and ownership, resource alignment, continuous monitoring and feedback, and agility and adaptability. Clear communication ensures that all employees understand their roles and how their work contributes to the overall strategy. Accountability and ownership foster a culture where individuals are responsible for their tasks and outcomes, ensuring that everyone is committed to achieving results. Resource alignment ensures that the organization has the necessary tools, budget, and personnel to meet its goals. Continuous monitoring and feedback help track progress, address obstacles, and make necessary adjustments to stay on course. Lastly, agility and adaptability allow the organization to pivot quickly in response to changes while maintaining focus on strategic objectives.

Importance in a Momentum Culture

Driving execution is essential because it ensures that strategies are not just plans on paper but are actively implemented and produce results. According to a Harvard Business Review study, companies that excel at execution are 70% more likely to outperform their peers financially. Execution aligns the organization, prevents strategic drift, and ensures efficient use of resources. Without effective execution, organizations risk inefficiencies and missed opportunities, as highlighted by the Project Management Institute's report, which found poor execution as the primary cause of 39% of project failures.

Momentum Culture Assessment - Driving Execution

In assessing an organization's ability to drive execution, we focus on evaluating how well leaders are developed around business acumen and strategic execution, whether the organization's structure supports execution while minimizing bureaucracy, and if the working structure is built around customer interactions rather than internal processes. The assessment aims to provide insights into the organization's execution capabilities, identifying strengths and areas for improvement to ensure that strategies are effectively translated into action and deliver the desired outcomes.

BUILD YOUR CULTURAL FLYWHEEL

1. *Foster Leadership Commitment*
    - Ensure that leaders are fully committed to driving execution. This includes setting clear expectations, providing necessary resources, and being actively involved in monitoring progress. Leadership's commitment to execution is crucial for setting the tone and pace across the organization.

2. *Develop Execution Capabilities*
    - Invest in training and developing the capabilities required for effective execution. Focus on project management, time management, and other skills essential for turning strategy into action. This ensures that employees are equipped with the tools they need to execute tasks efficiently.

3. *Establish a Culture of Accountability*
    - Create a culture that values execution by encouraging employees to take ownership of their work. Hold them accountable for their actions and reward them for achieving tangible results. This culture should promote collaboration, as execution often requires cross-functional teamwork.

4. *Align Incentives with Execution Goals*

- Align incentive structures with execution goals to motivate employees. Reward employees not just for effort but for the tangible outcomes they achieve. This alignment ensures that everyone is focused on driving the organization toward its strategic objectives.

By focusing on these practices, organizations can create a culture where execution is not just a priority but a core capability, driving sustained success and competitive advantage.

Resources

I have created a set of companion tools that can help you implement the concepts shared in the book. Here is a link to those tools:

FROM ALIGNMENT TO EXECUTION: HARNESSING THE POWER OF VECTOR

Throughout this chapter, we've examined how the elements of Coordinating Incentives and Driving Execution work together to form the backbone of Vector, ensuring that your cultural energy is directed with purpose and efficiency.

Coordinating Incentives has shown us the importance of connecting individual motivations and team goals to the organization's broader vision and strategy. This alignment ensures that every effort, every action, and every reward is directly contributing to the strategic objectives that define success. It fosters a sense of shared purpose across the organization, turning disparate actions into a cohesive movement toward common goals.

Driving Execution is the catalyst that transforms strategic intent into measurable outcomes. It emphasizes the importance of structuring your organization around the key drivers of value creation and minimizing bureaucratic friction that gets in the way of your people focusing on those key drivers.

While each of these Dynamics are important, they are also highly interdependent. One of the most insidious impediments to reliable execution is the issue of incentives. When I work with clients to help them drive execution in a specific area of their business, I often find that workers are being incentivized – either overtly or subtly – to take actions that are either in direct opposition, or at least orthogonal, to the desired behavior. Some of the issues are in broad daylight, and you wonder how the organization allowed the confusion. But most are insidious, and you would never find them without real digging. Most misdirection comes from unwritten cultural norms that have never been rooted out. Interviews and focus groups are the most reliable ways to find these issues, as they will often not show up in surveys or under direct inquiry. When you can't figure out why something just isn't working, it is often a very human factor, and humans are driven by incentives.

The Vector property is designed to ensure that the energy you created in Fusion is not wasted, but carefully channeled to maximize impact and minimize waste. But that energy must also be accelerated to achieve the velocity required for beating the competition. This is where the next element of the Momentum Culture framework comes into play: Velocity. It adds the final component, an approach to leadership based on Empowerment & Accountability, and effective Decision Making.

In the next section, we'll delve into how empowering employees, fostering accountability, and mastering decision-making can drive your organization to new heights. Join us as we continue this journey, unlocking the final piece of the Momentum Culture framework and setting the stage for sustained, competitive advantage.

VELOCITY

Physics velocity - phys·ics ve·loc·i·ty - /'fiziks və'läsədē/

The speed of an object in a given direction. In physics, velocity is a vector quantity, meaning it includes both the speed of an object and the direction in which it is moving.

Cultural velocity - cul·tur·al ve·loc·i·ty - /'kəlCH(ə)rəl və'läsədē/

The pace at which an organization's culture moves toward its strategic goals. It ensures that the momentum generated within the organization is accelerated efficiently toward meaningful outcomes.

16

VELOCITY

From Strategy to Success: How Cultural Velocity Accelerates Results

In the Momentum Culture framework, Velocity is the force that transforms strategic vision into tangible success by ensuring that your organization moves quickly and decisively toward its goals. Velocity is where the cultural energy generated by Fusion, and directed by Vector, gains the speed you need to outpace the competition. This chapter delves into the concept of Cultural Velocity, the pace and direction at which your organization's culture drives strategic execution. It's about moving faster, working smarter, and achieving better results by creating a culture that prioritizes execution and accountability.

The Elements of Velocity: Empowerment & Accountability and Organizational Decision-Making

At the heart of Velocity are two critical components: Empowerment & Accountability and Organizational Decision-Making. These elements work together to ensure that your organization's momentum is accelerated, pushing your team towards strategic goals with urgency and precision.

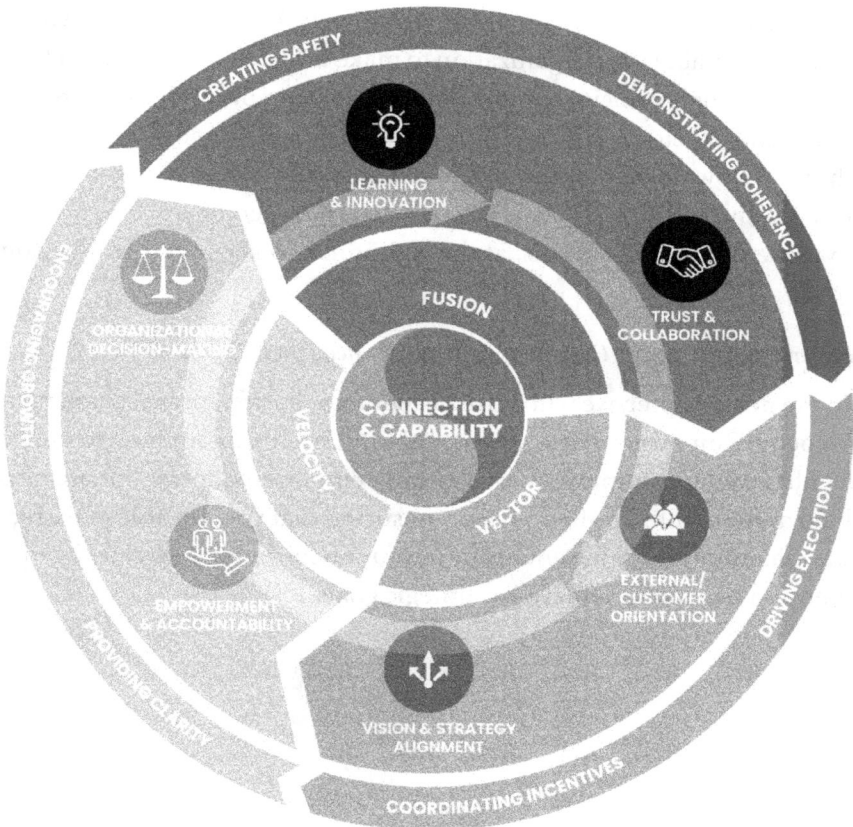

Empowerment & Accountability is about creating a culture where individuals are both empowered to act and held accountable for the results, in equal measures. It's the delicate balance between giving your employees the autonomy they need to innovate and make decisions, while also ensuring that they are responsible for the outcomes of those decisions. This balance is crucial for driving swift and effective execution. When employees feel empowered, they are more likely to take ownership of their work and make decisions that align with the organization's strategic goals. Accountability ensures that these actions are measured, and that there is a clear connection between performance and results, fostering a culture of high performance and continuous improvement.

Organizational Decision-Making focuses on the processes and structures that enable your organization to make decisions quickly and effectively. In a high-velocity culture, decision-making processes are streamlined and efficient, minimizing bureaucracy and removing obstacles that can slow down progress. It's about ensuring that your organization is agile and responsive, ensuring that the right people are empowered to make the right decisions, at the right time, to keep your strategy on track.

Faster, Smarter, Better: How Velocity Turns Strategy into Success

In the next chapter, we will delve deeper into the first critical element of Velocity: Empowerment & Accountability. We'll explore how to create a culture where employees are not only empowered to act but are also held accountable for their actions, ensuring that you are able to extract the maximum available energy from your organization to create the momentum needed to achieve its strategic goals.

17
EMPOWERMENT & ACCOUNTABILITY

Coaching as the Catalyst: Building a Balanced Culture of Empowerment and Accountability

In high-performing cultures, true leadership is less about giving directives and more about fostering growth through allowing employees the freedom and responsibility to maximize their potential. Empowerment and accountability, the twin pillars of effective leadership, are deeply intertwined—one cannot exist without the other. Coaching can act as the catalyst that binds these two critical elements together, ensuring that employees are not only equipped to make decisions but are also prepared to take full responsibility for the outcomes.

As we explore this chapter, we will dive into how coaching acts as the cornerstone of a culture that balances empowerment and accountability. We'll examine the key principles that make coaching effective and how this approach can transform leadership dynamics, ensuring that your organization thrives in today's competitive landscape.

Things You Will Learn in This Chapter:

- *The Power of Coaching is Empowerment:* Understand how coaching empowers employees by giving them the tools, confidence, and autonomy to make decisions, leading to increased innovation, productivity, and engagement.

- *The Feedback Fallacy and Its Impact on Accountability:* Explore the concept of the feedback fallacy and why traditional feedback methods often fail to build true accountability. Learn how coaching, rather than conventional feedback, fosters a culture where employees take ownership of their outcomes.

- *Building a Balanced Culture:* Discover the intricate relationship between empowerment and accountability in creating a Momentum Culture. Learn how these elements must be balanced through effective coaching to drive sustainable business performance.

- *Practical Coaching Strategies:* Gain insights into specific coaching techniques that leaders can use to enhance both empowerment and accountability within their teams, ensuring that employees are aligned with the organization's goals and values.

Exploring the Connection Between Empowerment and Accountability

Empowerment and accountability are two sides of the same coin in a high-performing organization. They are intrinsically linked, each reinforcing and enabling the other in a way that drives both individual and organizational success.

Empowerment: A Catalyst for Ownership

Empowerment in the workplace refers to the process of giving employees the autonomy, resources, and authority to make decisions and take actions on their own. This empowerment is crucial for fostering innovation, creativity, and agility within an organization. When employees feel empowered, they are more likely to take initiative, experiment with new ideas, and push the boundaries of what is possible. They feel a sense of ownership over their work, which leads to greater engagement and satisfaction.

However, empowerment without accountability can lead to chaos and inconsistency. Without a framework of accountability, empowered employees might take actions that are misaligned with organizational goals, leading to wasted resources and missed opportunities.

Accountability: The Framework for Responsible Action

Accountability ensures that the empowerment given to employees translates into responsible and effective action. It means that employees are not just free to make decisions but are also answerable for the outcomes of those decisions. Accountability provides the structure within which empowerment can flourish. It sets clear expectations, defines the parameters for decision-making, and ensures that actions are aligned with the organization's strategic objectives.

Without empowerment, accountability can feel oppressive and stifling. Employees may feel micromanaged, leading to disengagement and a lack of initiative. Conversely, accountability without empowerment can result in a punitive culture where employees are held responsible for outcomes without being given the authority or resources to influence those outcomes effectively.

The Synergy: Balancing Empowerment and Accountability

In a Momentum Culture, empowerment and accountability must be balanced to create an environment where employees feel both supported and responsible. Empowerment drives employees to innovate and take ownership of their work, while accountability ensures that their actions contribute to the organization's goals.

Coaching plays a pivotal role in maintaining this balance. Effective coaching helps employees understand their roles and responsibilities and allows them to make the best choices on how to align their actions with the organization's strategic goals.

The Challenges of Achieving Balance

Achieving the right balance between empowerment and accountability is not without its challenges. Leaders must resist the temptation to micromanage, which can undermine empowerment. At the same time, they must avoid being too hands-off, which can result in a lack of accountability. The key is strong coaching skills, applied consistently.

This balance is critical to building a Momentum Culture, where employees are motivated, engaged, and aligned with the organization's vision and strategy. When empowerment and accountability are in harmony, the organization benefits from a workforce that is both innovative and disciplined, driving sustainable success.

RESEARCH ON THE IMPACT OF EMPOWERMENT & ACCOUNTABILITY ON CULTURE

The Role of Coaching in Balancing Empowerment and Accountability

Research into high-performing cultures revealed that the relationship between these two elements is pivotal in determining the health and momentum of an organization[17]. Aside from our own research, material from third parties consistently highlighted coaching as a critical factor in balancing empowerment and accountability[18]. Effective coaching practices were strongly correlated with perceptions of a positive and balanced culture.

One prominent example comes from Google's internal studies, where data-driven insights showed that the quality of management had a significant impact on employee performance and retention[19]. Coaching emerged as one of the most critical skills that separated high-performing managers from the rest. Google found that managers who excelled at coaching improved team performance and employee satisfaction and engagement.

Similarly, our own research within various organizations confirmed that coaching is a linchpin for creating a culture where empowerment and accountability thrive. Employees in environments where coaching was prevalent reported more positive attitudes toward their corporate culture. Employees who believe that their manager is a good coach was the top predicting element in this factor that predicted strong cultural momentum.

> *"Provide more coaching, enable employees' growth, minimize micro-managing."*

—Research Responses

---

[17] (The Leadership Coaches, n.d.)
[18] (Theeboom, 2014)
[19] (Garvin, 2013)

Perception of Leadership Accountability is Key

A crucial finding in our research was that the perception of leadership accountability was the number one driver of a healthy balance between empowerment and accountability. Employees are more likely to embrace accountability when they see their leaders doing the same. This perception is tied to a culture of fairness and transparency—when leaders are held accountable for their actions and decisions, to a degree that is similar to that for front-line employees, it sets a powerful example for the rest of the organization.

In high-momentum cultures, leadership accountability is visible and consistent. Leaders demonstrate ownership of both successes and failures, and this behavior cascades down through the ranks, fostering a culture where employees feel empowered to take responsibility for their actions. On the other hand, in cultures where employees perceive a double standard—where leaders are not held to the same level of accountability—the balance is disrupted, leading to disengagement and mistrust.

> **"I would like to see leaders take in feedback as they give out feedback."**
> —Research Responses

The Importance of Fair and Realistic Expectations

Another key insight was the importance of setting fair and realistic expectations. Not surprisingly, our research found that when employees perceive that the goals set for them are achievable and that timelines are reasonable, they are more likely to take ownership of their tasks and deliver high-quality results. Conversely, in environments where expectations are perceived as unrealistic or arbitrary, empowerment becomes meaningless, and accountability feels punitive. This disconnect can lead to a breakdown in trust and a significant drop in morale and productivity. High-performing cultures ensure that empowerment is coupled with support and that accountability is fair and based on well-communicated expectations.

Differential Rewards and Recognition Are Essential

A pervasive weakness identified in many organizations was the lack of differential rewards and recognition for employees who perform above expectations. Our research showed that when high performance is not adequately recognized and rewarded, it undermines the very foundation of accountability. Employees are less likely to push themselves or take ownership of challenging tasks if they do not see a clear link between their efforts and tangible rewards.

> *"Transparent rewards for good performance that creates results."*
—Research Responses

In Momentum Cultures, rewards and recognition are used strategically to reinforce the connection between empowerment and accountability. Employees who demonstrate initiative and responsibility are celebrated, and this recognition serves as a powerful motivator for others. However, it is not just about the rewards; it's about ensuring that these rewards are perceived as fair and directly tied to the behaviors and outcomes that align with the organization's goals.

EXPLORING EMPOWERMENT IN MOMENTUM CULTURES

In this section, we explore what true empowerment looks like, its impact on organizational culture, and how it can be effectively implemented and sustained.

The Essence of Empowerment

Empowerment in a Momentum Culture is rooted in trust. It begins with the belief that employees are capable, intelligent, and resourceful individuals who can make significant contributions to the organization's success. This belief is actively demonstrated through the delegation of authority, provision of resources, and encouragement of independent decision-making.

Empowered employees are more likely to go above and beyond their job descriptions because they feel personally invested in the outcomes of their efforts. They do not simply execute tasks; they innovate, solve problems, and drive the organization forward.

The Impact of Empowerment on Organizational Culture

Empowerment is a key driver of positive connection to organizational culture. When employees are given the autonomy to make decisions and act, they develop a stronger connection to their coworkers and the organization.

Moreover, empowerment leads to a more agile and responsive organization. Empowered employees can quickly adapt to changes, seize opportunities, and respond to challenges without waiting for approval from higher-ups. This agility is particularly important in today's fast-paced business environment, where the ability to pivot quickly can be a significant competitive advantage.

In our research, we found that organizations with high levels of empowerment also tend to have high levels of innovation. When employees are trusted to experiment and take risks, they are more likely to come up with creative solutions and new ideas that drive the business forward. This culture of innovation is essential for maintaining momentum and staying ahead of the competition.

Challenges of Empowerment

On the other hand, empowerment without accountability can lead to chaos, where employees act without considering the consequences of their decisions. Therefore, it is crucial to pair empowerment with clear expectations and accountability mechanisms to ensure that empowered employees are also responsible for their actions and outcomes.

CASE EXAMPLE: PEOPLE'S EXPRESS AIRLINE

One of the most powerful examples of empowerment in action from my interviews with senior executives comes from People's Express Airline. Bob Parsons, a former employee of the airline, shared his early career experience of working in an environment that truly embraced empowerment. People's Express was known for hiring employees based on mindset and skills rather than prior experience. The airline focused on selecting individuals who could function well with autonomy – people who were positive, collaborative, and had a servant-leader mentality.

At People's Express, employees were given broad latitude to solve problems on behalf of customers. They were empowered to make decisions without needing to escalate issues to higher-ups. In many ways, it was similar to the famous "$2,000 rule" at Ritz Carlton, where employees can spend up to $2,000 to resolve a customer issue without managerial approval. This level of trust and autonomy created a strong bond between employees, the organization, and most importantly, their customers - fostering a culture of ownership and commitment.

Parsons recalled how this empowerment made him feel deeply connected to the company, a feeling that has stayed with him for over three decades. Although People's Express eventually went out of business due to strategic missteps, the culture of empowerment it created left a lasting impression on its employees. This case highlights the power of empowerment in creating a motivated, engaged, and loyal workforce.

LEVERAGE POINT:

- Allow individuals the freedom to use their initiative to solve problems on their own to build connection through trust.

THE PREVALENCE OF MICROMANAGEMENT AND THE FEEDBACK FALLACY

The opposite of the autonomy that Parsons shared from his experience from People's Express, is an overcontrolling level of micromanagement. If empowering employees were straightforward, every organization would be doing it successfully. Yet, many leaders struggle with letting go of control, leading to a culture where micromanagement, often disguised as feedback, prevails.

> *"Give people space to perform and apply their knowledge and skills, and do not micromanage."*
>
> —Research Responses

Why is Micromanagement So Prevalent?

Micromanagement frequently arises from a combination of experience and the perceived efficiency of providing direct answers rather than guiding employees to find solutions themselves. Senior managers, with their wealth of experience, often see a clear path forward. This clarity can make it difficult for them to resist stepping in, especially when they believe they can expedite the process by providing direct instructions. However, while it may seem more efficient in the short term, micromanagement comes at a significant cost. It stifles creativity, erodes trust, and diminishes employees' sense of ownership in solving problems – settling for a "wait for someone to tell me what to do" mindset.

The Feedback Fallacy: A Common Misstep

Micromanagement often masquerades as feedback, particularly in organizations where feedback is emphasized as a crucial component of performance management. However, as Marcus Buckingham and Ashley Goodall argue in their book "9 Lies About Work," this traditional approach to feedback is fundamentally flawed—a concept they term the "Feedback Fallacy."

The Feedback Fallacy suggests that feedback often reflects more about the person giving it than the person receiving it. It's frequently based on the giver's subjective perceptions, which can be biased and may not accurately reflect the reality of the situation. When feedback focuses heavily on negative aspects, it can demoralize and disengage employees, making them feel undervalued and fostering a culture of fear where mistakes are hidden rather than addressed constructively.

The Pitfalls of Negative Feedback

Negative feedback tends to zero in on what an employee is doing wrong, rather than recognizing what they are doing right. This approach can create a demotivating environment, leading to a reduction in morale and productivity. Employees who are consistently criticized may become more risk-averse, avoiding innovation for fear of further criticism.

> *"Focus on more positive contributions and impacts to the business rather than dwell or focus on the negative issues."*

—Research Responses

Moreover, this type of feedback can cause employees to disengage from their work and the organization. When the focus is on weaknesses rather than strengths, employees may feel that their contributions are not appreciated, which can lead to a decrease in job satisfaction and commitment.

Shifting from Feedback to Coaching

The alternative to the traditional feedback model is a coaching approach that emphasizes positive reinforcement and the development of strengths. By shifting from a feedback-focused culture to one centered on coaching, managers can help employees recognize their strengths and leverage them more effectively. This approach not only boosts confidence but also fosters a deeper connection between the employee and the organization.

In a coaching culture, leaders ask questions that prompt self-reflection and encourage employees to think about how they can use their strengths to overcome challenges. This method is aligned with the ethos of a Momentum Culture leader, who guides their team through inquiry rather than directives. Coaching becomes a discipline built on helping individuals identify their own challenges and discover their own solutions.

By adopting this approach, leaders can minimize the prevalence of micromanagement, instead fostering a culture of empowerment where employees feel trusted, valued, and motivated to contribute to the organization's success.

EXPLORING ACCOUNTABILITY IN MOMENTUM CULTURES

Accountability is the counterbalance to empowerment within a Momentum Culture. While empowerment gives employees the autonomy to make decisions and act, accountability ensures that these decisions and actions are aligned with the organization's goals and standards. It is the mechanism through which empowerment is channeled into meaningful, productive outcomes.

The Essence of Accountability

In a Momentum Culture, accountability is not about assigning blame or enforcing compliance; rather, it is about fostering a sense of ownership and responsibility. When employees are held accountable, they understand that they are responsible for both the successes and failures of their decisions. This understanding drives them to act with greater care, diligence, and commitment.

Accountability also involves setting clear expectations and standards. Employees need to know what is expected of them and how their performance will be measured. This clarity helps them align their actions with the organization's objectives and ensures that their efforts contribute to the overall success of the business.

Moreover, accountability is about fairness and consistency. It requires leaders to apply the same standards to everyone, including themselves. When employees see that their leaders are also held accountable, it builds trust and reinforces the culture of ownership within the organization.

The Role of Leaders in Driving Accountability

Leaders play a crucial role in establishing and maintaining a culture of accountability. They set the tone by modeling the behavior they expect from others. This means that leaders must not only hold their teams accountable but also hold themselves accountable for their actions and decisions.

One of the key responsibilities of a leader is to create an environment where accountability is seen as a positive force, not punitive. This involves externalizing problems and problem-solving approaches – helping workers identify incorrect logic or bad processes instead of communicating that they are bad.

In addition, leaders must establish clear structures and processes for accountability. This includes setting measurable goals, providing regular updates on progress, and creating a system for recognizing and rewarding those who meet or exceed expectations. Consistent application of these structures and processes help to embed accountability into the daily operations of the organization and ensure that it is consistently applied across all levels.

The Dangers of a Lack of Accountability

A lack of accountability can have serious consequences for an organization. Without accountability, there is no mechanism to ensure that employees are meeting their responsibilities or contributing to the organization's goals. This can lead to a culture of complacency, where underperformance is tolerated, and high standards are not upheld.

Moreover, a lack of accountability can erode trust within the organization. When employees see that others are not held accountable for their actions, it creates a sense of unfairness and resentment. This can lead to disengagement, decreased morale, and ultimately, higher turnover.

In contrast, a strong culture of accountability creates a sense of fairness and transparency. It ensures that everyone is held to the same standards and that those who meet or exceed expectations are recognized and rewarded.

CASE EXAMPLE: FREESCALE'S SEMICONDUCTOR

The Challenge

In the early 2000s, Freescale Semiconductor's manufacturing unit faced a daunting challenge. Amidst a competitive landscape where chip foundries were consolidating and achieving economies of scale, the unit's declining quality, yield, and margin performance threatened its viability. Despite individual team efforts, the overall performance remained stagnant. Recognizing that it was a systemic issue, Brett Rodgers, the HR head, and Alex Pepe, the unit's Global VP, sought to instill a culture of accountability.

Solution

Inspired by the principles outlined in William R. Daniels and John G. Mathers' "The Change-ABLE Organization," Rodgers and Pepe implemented a radical team restructuring. Instead of focusing on individual goals, teams were aligned to their managers' expected outcomes. This shift created a clear line of accountability, where each team's success was directly linked to the performance of the entire unit. Managers were held accountable for their teams' success or failure, ensuring that alignment and accountability were embedded into the system.

To further enhance collaboration and problem-solving, meetings were restructured to focus on resolving issues escalated by teams, complete with their recommendations. This empowered teams to take ownership of their work and contribute to the unit's overall success.

Outcomes

The impact of these changes was profound. Employees gained a clear understanding of their roles and responsibilities, eliminating confusion and fostering a culture of collaboration and shared ownership. Teams became more engaged, raising suggestions and contributing to decision-making. The results were remarkable: quality, yield, and margin metrics soared, far surpassing initial targets. This turnaround was instrumental in Freescale's successful recovery and eventual $17B purchase in 2006 by a private equity group led by the Blackstone Group[20]. Up to that point, it was the largest ever buyout of a technology company, demonstrating the power of accountability as a cornerstone of organizational success.

LEVERAGE POINT:

1. Consider the idea of team goals. The alignment and camaraderie you create could be transformational.

ACCOUNTABILITY AND RECOGNITION

Accountability is closely linked to recognition and rewards. In a Momentum Culture, it is not enough to hold employees accountable; it is also essential to recognize and reward those who meet or exceed expectations. This recognition reinforces the behavior you want to see and motivates others to strive for the same level of performance.

---

[20] Invalid source specified.

However, it is important to reward the right behaviors, not just the outcomes. For example, if a team achieves its goals but does so by cutting corners or engaging in unethical behavior, rewarding them could send the wrong message. Instead, recognition should be based on both the results and the way those results were achieved.

This approach ensures that accountability is not just about meeting targets but also about upholding the organization's values and standards. It creates a culture where employees are motivated to do their best work while also maintaining the organization's integrity. Coaching can be a valuable tool to help you do that.

ENHANCING ACCOUNTABILITY THROUGH COACHING

Coaching plays a pivotal role in creating a culture of accountability within an organization. I often see leaders take one of three different approaches to coaching people who are not getting the desired results.

Results-Based Coaching focuses primarily on the outcomes that employees achieve. Many leaders pride themselves on their single-mindedness to results, championing quotes like this one from football coach, Bill Parcells:

> *"You don't get any medal for trying something, you get medals for results."*

While results are important, this approach can sometimes reinforce the wrong behaviors. For example, an employee might achieve a positive outcome through unethical means or by sheer luck, which can inadvertently reward the wrong actions. Conversely, a negative outcome might occur from a purely extrinsic factor despite an employee's best efforts and sound decision-making, leading to unfair punishment.

Results-Based Coaching tends to prioritize the end result over the process, which can undermine the development of sustainable, successful behaviors. It's a reactive approach that focuses on what has already happened, rather than proactively shaping the behaviors that lead to consistent success.

Behavior-Based Coaching delves deeper into the actions that led to the results. This approach helps employees connect their behaviors to the outcomes they produce. When a manager coaches an employee based on the behaviors they exhibited, they help the employee understand what specific actions led to success or failure – "when you did this, it led to that".

This method is more constructive than purely results-based coaching, as it builds a stronger foundation for future performance by reinforcing positive behaviors. However, it may still fall short if it doesn't address the underlying thought processes that drive those behaviors.

Cognitive-Based Coaching goes a step further by exploring the thought processes and decision-making frameworks that guide an employee's actions. This approach begins with the outcome and traces back to the cognitive processes that influenced the employee's decisions and behavior. By using a structured inquiry process, I sometimes refer to as "The 5 What's and a How," coaches can help employees identify where their logic or perceptions may have been flawed.

For example, a coach might ask:

- **What** was your description of the situation?
- **What** was the core problem you identified, and how did it make you feel?
- **What** actions did you take?
- **What** did you see that suggested those actions would be most effective?
- **What** did you think would happen as a result of those actions?

This method allows employees to see where their cognitive processes might have gone astray, enabling them to adjust their thinking and approach for the future. It shifts the narrative from "you made a mistake" to "let's understand where the logic broke down," which is a far more empowering and constructive way to hold someone accountable.

Cognitive-Based Coaching is powerful because it not only addresses the specific situation at hand but also equips employees with the tools to think more critically and strategically in future situations. It transforms accountability from a punitive measure into a developmental process that drives continuous improvement.

By focusing not just on results, but on the behaviors and thought processes that lead to those results, leaders can foster a deeper sense of ownership and responsibility in their teams. This approach ensures that empowerment is directed towards meaningful, repeatable outcomes that align with the organization's goals and values.

REDEFINING LEADERSHIP FOR EMPOWERMENT AND ACCOUNTABILITY

To cultivate a culture of empowerment and accountability, managers must adopt a leadership style that maximizes the potential of their team members. Liz Wiseman, in her influential book "Multipliers: How the Best Leaders Make Everyone Smarter,[21]" provides valuable insights into how leaders can get the best out of their teams by fostering an environment that encourages autonomy, innovation, and ownership.

Wiseman's work leverages the core ideas of a coaching style of leadership, highlighting the importance of leaders who amplify the capabilities of their team members rather than stifling them. The essence of this leadership approach is to believe in the inherent intelligence and potential of employees, creating a culture where they feel empowered to take initiative, think critically, and solve problems independently.

---

[21] (Wiseman, 2010)

Shifting Leadership Mindsets

For leaders to make a shift to a coaching style of leadership, changes to both mindset and behavior are necessary:

1. *From Providing Answers to Asking Questions:* Rather than giving directives, leaders should focus on asking insightful questions that prompt their team members to think critically and develop their own solutions. This approach empowers employees and fosters a culture of innovation.

2. *From Controlling to Empowering:* Leaders must learn to trust their team members and resist the urge to control every aspect of their work. Empowerment means giving people the autonomy to make decisions and the accountability to own the results, both good and bad.

3. *From Knowing It All to Knowing Their People:* Effective leaders take the time to understand the strengths and weaknesses of their team members. They align tasks with individual strengths, thereby increasing the likelihood of success and fostering a sense of ownership.

4. *From Micro to Macro Management:* Leaders should focus on the bigger picture, allowing their team members to handle the details. They provide the necessary resources and support but do not interfere with execution unless absolutely necessary.

5. *From Scarcity to Abundance:* Leaders should operate from an abundance mindset, believing there is enough to go around, which encourages sharing, collaboration, and open communication.

By adopting these shifts, leaders can transform their management approach, creating a culture where empowerment and accountability are balanced, and where employees feel motivated to contribute their best work.

MAKING THE SHIFT TO MOMENTUM CULTURE OF EMPOWERMENT & ACCOUNTABILITY

For Organizations:

In a Momentum Culture centered around Empowerment and Accountability, the organization actively cultivates a culture where ownership and reliability are fundamental. Processes and capabilities are designed to empower employees, fostering a deep sense of responsibility and trust. By embedding coaching and goal setting into everyday practices, and by utilizing tools like performance dashboards and recognition systems, the organization ensures that accountability is both encouraged and rewarded. This environment supports continuous improvement and values the contributions of every employee, reinforcing a shared commitment to success.

For Individuals:

In a Momentum Culture of Empowerment and Accountability, individuals are deeply committed to taking ownership of their actions and outcomes. They approach their work with integrity, knowing that their decisions are trusted by the organization. Empowered to work autonomously and supported through ongoing coaching, employees strive to meet and exceed their goals. They believe in lifting others up and contributing to a culture of continuous improvement, confident that their efforts are recognized and celebrated within the organization.

MOMENTUM CULTURE MODEL FOR EMPOWERMENT AND ACCOUNTABILITY

Individuals	Organizations
Behaviors	**Processes & Capabilities**

Extrinsic

Individuals	Organizations
• **Takes Ownership:** Consistently takes responsibility for actions, outcomes, and the success of projects or tasks. • **Seeks Autonomy:** Actively seeks opportunities to work independently and make decisions within their scope of responsibility. • **Sets Clear Expectations:** Ensures that expectations are clearly communicated, understood, and aligned with the organization's goals. • **Provides and Accepts Coaching:** Regularly engages in coaching, both offering and receiving it, to develop skills, build confidence, and enhance decision-making abilities. • **Demonstrates Reliability:** Consistently meets commitments and delivers on promises, building trust with colleagues and leaders.	• **Ownership Culture Development:** The organization fosters a culture where taking ownership is encouraged and rewarded, ensuring employees feel responsible for their work and outcomes. • **Coaching Culture Implementation:** The organization embeds coaching as a core part of its culture, providing continuous opportunities for employees to receive and offer coaching. • **Empowerment through Trust:** The organization builds trust with employees by empowering them with the autonomy and resources needed to excel in their roles. • **Goal Setting and Tracking:** The organization supports employees in setting clear, measurable goals and provides tools to track progress, ensuring accountability for achieving results. • **Recognition and Reward Systems:** The organization recognizes and rewards employees who consistently demonstrate ownership, reliability, and alignment with organizational expectations.

Intrinsic

Skills

- **Self-Management:** The ability to manage one's time, priorities, and resources effectively, ensuring that tasks are completed efficiently and to a high standard.
- **Goal Setting:** Skill in setting clear, achievable goals that align with the organization's objectives.
- **Coaching:** The ability to both provide and receive coaching, using it as a tool for continuous development and performance improvement.
- **Accountability:** The ability to hold oneself and others accountable for meeting commitments and achieving goals.

Structures & Resources

- **Coaching Platforms:** Digital platforms that facilitate ongoing coaching interactions between employees and managers, and possibly external coaches, ensuring continuous development and support.
- **Performance Tracking Dashboards:** Real-time dashboards that allow employees and managers to track progress toward goals, ensuring accountability and transparency.
- **Recognition Systems:** Digital systems that allow for peer-to-peer and manager-to-employee recognition, celebrating individuals who consistently demonstrate ownership and reliability.
- **Reward and Incentive Programs:** Structured programs that reward employees for achieving their goals and demonstrating consistent ownership and accountability.

Mindsets

- **Ownership:** I believe that taking responsibility for my actions and outcomes is essential to my success, and I approach the world with a sense of ownership over my work.
- **Integrity:** I believe that acting with honesty and ensuring my actions are congruent with my commitments is essential for true accountability, and I approach the world with a commitment to integrity.
- **Empowerment of Others:** I believe that empowering others to succeed is just as important as my own empowerment, and I approach the world with a mindset of lifting others up.

Values

- **Trust:** We value trust as the foundation of empowerment, believing that employees who are trusted will rise to the occasion and perform at their best.
- **Continuous Improvement:** We believe in continuously striving for improvement and growth, both individually and organizationally, to achieve excellence.
- **Recognition:** We believe in recognizing and celebrating the achievements and contributions of our employees, reinforcing the importance of ownership and accountability.

Perception

" "I believe that by taking ownership of my actions and outcomes, I contribute meaningfully to the success of my projects and the organization. I am empowered to make decisions within my scope, and I value the opportunities for continuous development through coaching. I feel trusted by my organization, and I am committed to acting with integrity and reliability, knowing that my efforts are recognized and rewarded."

"We believe that fostering a culture of ownership and accountability is essential to achieving our strategic goals. By empowering our employees with the autonomy, resources, and trust they need, we create an environment where responsibility and reliability are valued. We are committed to continuous improvement and recognize the contributions of those who consistently align with our values, ensuring that everyone is supported and celebrated for their dedication to our shared success."

BUILD YOUR CULTURE FLYWHEEL: EMPOWERMENT AND ACCOUNTABILITY

Here's how you can build a cultural flywheel that reinforces empowerment and accountability at every level.

Thought-Provoking Questions

1. Are your managers equipped with the skills and mindset needed to coach their teams effectively. Are they helping employees find their own solutions and develop their capabilities, or are they simply dictating what needs to be done?

2. Is micromanagement holding your culture back? Are leaders too involved in day-to-day tasks, thereby stifling employee autonomy and growth?

3. Reflect on whether your leaders truly empower their teams by trusting them with decision-making and responsibility, or if they inadvertently encourage dependency by not allowing employees to take ownership of their work.

Turning Thought into Action:

1. Provide leaders with training and tools to become effective coaches. This includes structured coaching programs, workshops, and ongoing support to ensure that coaching becomes a natural part of leadership.

2. Establish transparent processes that define what accountability looks like in your organization. This includes setting clear expectations, providing the necessary resources for success, and ensuring that accountability is consistently applied at all levels.

3. Give employees the autonomy to make decisions and take actions that align with organizational goals. Provide them with the resources and support they need to succeed and recognize their efforts through rewards and recognition programs.

4. Shift from a traditional feedback model to one that focuses on coaching and positive reinforcement. Recognize and reward the right behaviors that lead to success, and ensure that feedback is constructive, actionable, and aligned with employees' strengths.

By integrating these principles into your organization, you can build a flywheel that continuously reinforces a culture of empowerment and accountability, driving sustained momentum and long-term success.

Resources

I have created a set of companion tools that can help you implement the concepts shared in the book. Here is a link to those tools:

Conclusion

Empowerment and accountability are the Yin and Yang of leadership within a Momentum Culture. Like the ancient concept of Yin and Yang, these two forces are interdependent, each containing the seed of the other, and neither can exist in isolation if true organizational harmony is to be achieved. Empowerment without accountability can lead to chaos, while accountability without empowerment can stifle innovation and motivation. Only by balancing these elements can an organization create a culture of trust, responsibility, and continuous improvement.

Through effective coaching, leaders play a crucial role in maintaining this balance. Coaching empowers employees by helping them discover their own solutions and paths forward while also holding them accountable for the outcomes.

As we move into the next chapter on **Organizational Decision Making,** we'll explore how these principles of empowerment and accountability manifest in the decisions made across the organization.

18

DECISION MAKING

"Fortune Favors the Bold, Abandons the Timid... And Rewards the Fast"

In today's rapidly evolving business landscape, the ability to make swift and informed decisions is no longer just an operational necessity, it's a strategic imperative. While companies may have similar structures, resources, and talent, the true differentiator lies in how decisively and effectively they make decisions. In this race, speed is a key factor that can either propel a company ahead of its competitors or leave it behind, struggling to catch up. The winners are those who can navigate uncertainty with agility, making decisions that are not only timely but also strategically sound.

Organizational decision-making was identified as the second most critical factor correlated with employees perceiving their company as a high-performing entity. Yet, many organizations struggle with this crucial capability. Despite the availability of more data than ever before, decision-making processes have slowed down rather than sped up, creating a significant drag on performance.

This chapter will explore how to transform decision-making into a competitive advantage by embracing the speed and decisiveness that the current business environment demands. The road of business is indeed littered with "flat squirrels"—those who hesitated too long and failed to act. But with the right approach, your organization can avoid this fate and instead be rewarded for its bold and swift decisions.

What You Will Learn in This Chapter:

- *Understanding the Impact of Speed:* Learn why speed is critical in today's fast-paced business environment, and how being decisive can create a competitive advantage that outpaces even the best competition.

- *Building a Foundation of Good Process:* Understand the critical role of governance, process, and talent development in creating a robust decision-making culture. Learning how clear decision rights, structured processes, and targeted enablement can empower your organization to make high-quality decisions consistently.

- *The Hidden Costs of Ineffective Decision-Making:* Discover how poor decision-making processes can erode organizational efficiency, leading to wasted time, missed opportunities, and significant financial losses.

- *Recruiting for Excellence:* Identify the key skills and attributes needed to build a decision-making powerhouse within your organization, ensuring you have the right talent in place to drive strategic success.

THE CHALLENGE OF ORGANIZATIONAL DECISION-MAKING

Organizational decision-making is a critical yet often overlooked capability. Despite its importance, many companies struggle with making timely, high-quality decisions that drive business performance. Research shows that only about half of employees believe their organizations make effective decisions. Even fewer feel that these decisions are made in a timely manner, which can lead to missed opportunities, wasted resources, and a loss of competitive edge.

According to a study by Harvard Business Review, ineffective decision-making processes waste a significant amount of time and resources[22]. The average organization loses hundreds of millions of dollars

---

[22] (Hammond, 1998)

annually due to poor decision-making practices. This inefficiency is compounded by the complexity of modern business environments, where the volume of data available can overwhelm decision-makers, slowing down the process rather than speeding it up.

The Critical Nature of Decision-Making and Its Complexity

In today's fast-paced business environment, speed is of the essence. Decades ago, decision-making was slow due to a lack of data. Now, organizations are awash in information, yet decision-making processes have not necessarily improved. In fact, they have often become even slower as decision-makers struggle to sift through vast amounts of data to make informed choices.

The core complication lies in the multifaceted nature of decision-making as a capability. Effective decision-making requires not only strong governance and processes but also the right people with the necessary skills. The environment is changing faster than organizations can adapt, and the skills required to make quick, high-quality decisions are not always present. Furthermore, as Jeff Bezos famously said, "Most decisions should probably be made with somewhere around 70% of the information you wish you had. If you wait for 90%, in most cases, you're probably being slow." The challenge is balancing speed and quality with the scope and impact of the decisions being made.

CASE STUDY: THE COST OF INDECISION

At a 150-year-old consumer packaged goods company, decision-making had become a significant problem. The company had seen five years of flat earnings with no increase in shareholder value. Despite this stagnation, the management team did not turn over, and the only top-tier score in their employee engagement surveys was "I plan to stay at this company for a long time." The combination of the two indicated a complacent workforce that was stuck.

The company's employees consistently cited decision-making as a major issue in annual engagement surveys. They pointed to inconsistent processes, a lack of clarity around ownership and roles, and a tendency to wait for consensus as the primary challenges. Decisions were often made and then unmade, leading to significant delays and inefficiencies.

To address these issues, the company decided to invest in improving their decision-making capabilities and engaged my consulting team to provide recommendations. However, after several rounds of meetings, the final decision to kick off the project was postponed due to new stakeholders with conflicting goals joining the discussion. At last, it seemed like the team was in place and the project could commence. A meeting was called at the headquarters for final approval. After the meeting ran over an hour long, ultimately, they could not reach a decision on the project, and it was shelved. The company could not make a decision on a project to improve their decision making. Let that sink in.

This failure to make a timely decision not only delayed the necessary improvements but also left the company on a path of slower growth, delivering roughly half the overall return on invested capital of its closest competitor over the next decade.

In very simple terms, corporations are nothing but the sum of their decisions. So, if your organization cannot make decisions effectively, your shareholder value won't sum up to much.

LEVERAGE POINTS:

- Decision-making is a foundational capability within enterprises, and tends to define the organization, for better or worse. If you want a Momentum Culture, create clear processes and provide the training and tools needed for it to be core competence.

- Decision-making ineffectiveness is so pervasive across the competitive landscape, it represents an easy opportunity to build a sustainable advantage.

RESEARCH ON THE IMPACT OF DECISION MAKING ON CULTURE

The research findings underscore the crucial role decision-making plays in shaping an organization's culture and its perceived competence. In the Momentum Culture framework, decision-making emerged as the top driver influencing how employees view their company's overall effectiveness. The ability of an organization to identify issues and make timely decisions significantly impacts on employees' confidence in the company's leadership and direction. When organizations invest in enhancing their decision-making capabilities, employees interpret this as a serious commitment to long-term success.

Comments from employees reflected a strong emphasis on the need for enablement investments, particularly in meaningful training tailored to decision-making. This kind of training was seen as a clear indicator that the organization values sharpening decision-making as a core competency. Employees who feel their organization is dedicated to improving decision-making processes are more likely to trust the company's leadership and direction, resulting in a stronger, more positive cultural perception.

The research also identified a split in perceptions based on employees' experiences with their company's decision-making processes. Accelerators generally expressed positive sentiments but also wanted more clarity and standardization. These employees emphasized the importance of decentralizing decision-making, allowing decisions to be made closer to where the actual work is done. This feedback highlights the necessity of not only having a robust decision-making process but also ensuring it is efficiently distributed throughout the organization.

> *"It'd be ideal to establish a stream-lined decision-making process that encourages cross-functional collaboration and that ensures timely execution. "*

—Research Responses

Conversely, Decelerators raised concerns about the transparency of decision-making processes. They reported dissatisfaction with the lack of clarity regarding who was making decisions and the rationale behind those decisions, leading to feelings of disempowerment and disengagement. This feedback highlights the critical need for clear communication and transparency to foster a positive culture and maintain employee engagement.

> *"Be more transparent and involve the employees in decisions."*

—Research Responses

KEY INSIGHTS:

Make Decisions Once

In Momentum Cultures, decisions are thoroughly debated before being finalized, rather than after the fact. This approach contrasts sharply with weaker cultures, where vacillation and uncertainty can lead to repeated loops of decision-making and a loss of execution speed—factors detrimental to organizational success.

Be Fundamentally Sound

Although decision-making is a critical capability, it is often taken for granted and not given the explicit focus it deserves. However, the research shows that simply having clear processes, good communication, and basic training in decision-making can set a company apart from its competitors.

Focus on Cross-Functional Decisions

While tactical decisions may not require extensive support, and major strategic decisions already receive significant attention, cross-functional operational decisions are often overlooked. These decisions, however, hold substantial leverage and can greatly impact an organization's momentum.

Decision-Making Requires Skills

Decision-making is a complex process requiring a blend of integrated skills, including critical thinking, pattern recognition, and creativity. Despite the importance of these skills, many organizations do not explicitly recruit for them, missing an opportunity to build a stronger, more agile decision-making culture.

In summary, the findings illustrate that decision-making should be embedded as a core organizational competency. By developing clear processes, ensuring transparent communication, and fostering the necessary skills across all levels, organizations can transform their decision-making processes into a significant competitive advantage. This shift not only enhances decision quality but also speeds up execution, positioning the organization for sustained success.

CASE EXAMPLE: GLOBAL PAPER COMPANY

Having explored the critical role of decision-making and the challenges that can arise when organizations struggle to make timely and effective decisions, let's now shift our focus to a positive example. This case study will illustrate how a company successfully navigated complex decision-making challenges to drive significant growth and organizational transformation.

The Challenge

In 2021, a Fortune 1000 US-based, global paper company faced an urgent need to redefine its business strategy due to geopolitical disruptions, particularly the impact of the war in Ukraine. With Russia being a major market, the company had to quickly adapt its business model to maintain its competitive edge and continue delivering value to its shareholders. But as company leadership had grown up within a 100-year-old, old school paper company before being spun out on its own, flexibility and speed wasn't their legacy.

The Solution

But, recognizing that they were operating in a new environment with different dynamics, company leadership took a bold approach. Rather than relying on established habits, rituals, and processes, they decided to rethink their decision-making framework entirely. They needed more speed, more decisions made closer to the business, and more flexibility in adapting to the changing environment. This fresh perspective allowed them to develop a regionalized strategy that was agile and responsive to the unique needs of individual countries.

The company began with an alignment meeting to clarify its "Main Thing". This clarity of purpose was essential in guiding all subsequent decisions. They established a singular focus on creating shareholder value, which became the cornerstone of their strategy and culture. Empowerment was central to their new approach, with decision-making authority pushed far down into the organization, ensuring that those closest to the work were empowered to act swiftly and decisively. Finally, training was provided to ensure that were clear processes and useful tools that would accelerate decision cycle time.

Outcomes

Company leadership also recognized the importance of maintaining alignment across the organization. There was no tolerance for a lack of alignment, and this commitment to unity helped drive a cohesive and effective decision-making process. The result was a company that, despite operating with many of the same people, had a radically different culture and decision-making approach. This transformation has been a key factor in Sylvamo's continued success and growth.

Through this case study, we see how Sylvamo exemplifies a Momentum Culture, where decision-making is leveraged as a competitive advantage. Their ability to adapt quickly, make high-quality decisions, and maintain alignment has positioned them for long-term success in a challenging and rapidly changing environment.

LEVERAGE POINT

- *"What got you here, won't get you there"* is a famous quote from Marshall Goldsmith reminds us that approaches that worked in other business environments will not necessarily work in the one you are currently in. Reassess the markets you are participating in and adjust your decision-making accordingly.

CREATING A COMPETITIVE ADVANTAGE THROUGH DECISION-MAKING

The core purpose of a Momentum Culture is to create a sustainable competitive advantage. One of the most powerful decision-making frameworks to help achieve this is the OODA Loop, conceptualized by John Boyd, a military strategist and US Air Force Colonel[23]. The OODA Loop—short for Observe, Orient, Decide, Act—is a decision-making cycle designed to accelerate the speed and quality of decisions, allowing an organization to outpace its competitors.

The OODA Loop and Decision-Making Speed

Boyd's OODA Loop emphasizes the importance of speed in decision-making as a strategic advantage. In a business context, the faster an organization can move through the OODA cycle, the more it forces

---

[23] (Boyd, n.d.)

competitors to react to situations that have already changed. This continuous adaptation is crucial in a rapidly evolving market landscape, where hesitation or indecision can be costly.

> *"The pilot who goes through the OODA cycle in the shortest time prevails because their opponent is caught responding to situations that have already changed."*

—Harry Hillaker, Chief Designer of the F-16

Hillaker is making the key point on how decision-making creates an opportunity for a sustainable competitive advantage. By processing decisions faster than the competition, you force your competition to react to you, not the other way around. Like the case example about FedEx, it fosters a proactive, offensive mentality, instead of a reactive, defensive one. To realize these advantages, you must master some basic organizational fundamentals.

Clarity in Governance and Decision-Making Processes

At the heart of effective decision-making is clarity. Organizations must establish clear governance structures that define who is responsible for making decisions, at what level, and under what circumstances. This clarity prevents decision paralysis and ensures that decisions are made by the people with the best information and the most relevant expertise.

Organizations should develop and communicate a consistent decision-making framework that everyone understands and follows. This framework should include processes for gathering data, analyzing options, and executing decisions. By standardizing these processes, organizations can reduce the time wasted on rehashing decisions and ensure that everyone is on the same page.

Empowerment Through Alignment

Empowerment is a critical element in a Momentum Culture, but it must be paired with alignment to be effective. Employees need to understand the organization's strategic goals and how their decisions contribute to achieving those goals. This alignment ensures that decisions made at all levels support the organization's overall direction and objectives.

> *"You've got to think about big things while you're doing small things, so that all the small things go in the right direction."*
>
> —Alvin Toffler

Empowered employees who are aligned with the company's vision are more likely to take initiative and make decisions that drive the organization forward. They understand the broader context and are equipped to act in ways that are consistent with the organization's values and goals.

Talent Development and Enablement

Effective decision-making requires a specific set of skills, including critical thinking, pattern recognition, and the ability to synthesize information quickly. Organizations must invest in developing these skills across their workforce through targeted training and development programs.

Focus on Recruiting

In addition to skill development, organizations should focus on recruiting individuals who naturally exhibit strong decision-making capabilities. Such people are not only good thinkers but also confident actors and collaborative team players. By building a talent base with these attributes, organizations can ensure that decision-making is a strength at all levels.

Creating a Culture of Speed and Quality

In a rapidly changing business environment, speed is often as important as the quality of decisions. Organizations must foster a culture where decisions are made quickly and confidently, but without sacrificing thoroughness and due diligence. This requires a balance between being fast and being right, which can be achieved through practice, feedback, and continuous improvement.

By implementing these shifts, organizations can transform their decision-making processes from a potential liability into a significant competitive advantage. They can become more agile, responsive, and effective in navigating the challenges of the modern business landscape.

MAKING THE SHIFT TO A MOMENTUM CULTURE OF DECISION-MAKING

For Organizations:

Shifting to a Momentum Culture of Decision-Making involves creating an environment where agility, empowerment, and strategic alignment are at the forefront. As an organization, this means fostering a culture where decisions are made quickly and confidently, supported by data and collaboration across departments. Employees are empowered to make decisions within their areas of responsibility, knowing that their choices are trusted and aligned with the broader strategic goals. The organization values continuous improvement, with regular reviews of past decisions to ensure learning and growth. This shift creates a dynamic, responsive organization that is agile in its decision-making and deeply committed to achieving its long-term objectives.

For Individuals:

Transitioning to a Momentum Culture of Decision-Making means embracing the responsibility and autonomy to make informed, strategic decisions that impact the organization's success. As an individual, you are encouraged to collaborate with others, seek diverse perspectives, and make decisions with confidence, knowing they align with the organization's strategic vision. This culture fosters a sense of accountability, where you are empowered to act quickly, supported by data and a clear understanding of the broader goals. You feel valued, trusted, and integral to the organization's success, as your decisions contribute to driving long-term, impactful outcomes.

MOMENTUM CULTURE MODEL OF DECISION-MAKING

Individuals	Organizations
Behaviors	**Processes & Capabilities**
• **Makes Timely Decisions:** Regularly makes decisions quickly and efficiently, ensuring that actions are taken without unnecessary delays. • **Follows a Structured Decision-Making Process:** Adheres to a systematic approach to making decisions, considering all relevant factors. • **Evaluates Risks and Benefits:** Thoroughly assesses potential risks and benefits before making decisions. • **Seeks Input from Relevant Stakeholders:** Actively involves the right stakeholders in the decision-making process to ensure all perspectives are considered. • **Communicates Decisions Clearly:** Ensures that decisions and their rationale are communicated effectively to all impacted parties.	• **Decision-Making Agility:** Fosters the ability to make timely decisions in a fast-paced environment, balancing speed with quality. • **Delegation Empowerment:** Empowers leaders and teams with the authority to make decisions within their areas of responsibility, fostering a culture of trust and accountability. • **Data-Driven Decision Support:** Provides tools and resources to support data-driven decision-making, ensuring that decisions are informed by accurate and relevant information. • **Cross-Functional Decision-Making Collaboration:** Encourages collaboration across departments in decision-making processes to ensure a holistic approach and alignment with organizational goals.

(Extrinsic)

Skills	Structures & Resources
• **Analytical Thinking:** Has the ability to analyze information and data to make well-informed decisions. • **Decisiveness:** Can make decisions confidently and quickly, even when information is incomplete. • **Data Interpretation:** Is proficient in interpreting data to inform decision-making and assess potential outcomes.	• **Decision-Making Frameworks:** Builds standardized frameworks that guide the decision-making process, ensuring consistency, thoroughness, and alignment with organizational goals. • **Decision-Making Training Programs:** Conducts comprehensive training programs designed to enhance employees' decision-making skills, including critical thinking, risk assessment, and strategic alignment. • **Recruiting for Decision-Making Skills:** Recruits candidates with strong decision-making abilities, ensuring that the organization is staffed with individuals capable of making sound decisions. • **Decision Execution Support Systems:** Employs tools and resources that assist in the effective execution of decisions, ensuring that once a decision is made, it is implemented efficiently and effectively. • **Decision Review and Learning Sessions:** Regularly schedules sessions where past decisions are reviewed, and lessons are learned, fostering a culture of continuous improvement in decision-making.

Intrinsic

Mindsets	Values
• **Collaboration:** I believe that diverse perspectives lead to better decisions, and I approach the world with a commitment to seeking input from others. • **Accountability:** I believe that being accountable for the outcomes of decisions is essential, and I approach the world with a strong sense of responsibility. • **Strategic Thinking:** I believe that every decision should align with the organization's broader strategy, and I approach the world with a focus on long-term impact.	• **Empowerment:** We value empowering employees at all levels to make decisions within their areas of responsibility, fostering a culture of trust and autonomy. • **Agility:** We value the ability to make timely decisions in a fast-paced environment, balancing speed with quality to stay ahead in the market. • **Strategic Alignment:** We believe that all decisions should be aligned with the organization's long-term vision and strategic goals, ensuring that every choice contributes to our broader objectives.
Perception	
"I believe that in this organization, my input is valued, and my decisions are trusted. I am empowered to make timely, well-informed decisions that align with our strategic goals, and I feel accountable for the outcomes. Collaboration is encouraged, and I know that my decisions contribute to the long-term success of the organization."	"We believe in empowering our employees to make informed, timely decisions that are aligned with our strategic goals. Our culture fosters trust, agility, and collaboration, ensuring that every decision made across the organization contributes to our broader objectives and long-term success."

BUILD YOUR CULTURE FLYWHEEL: DECISION-MAKING

Creating a culture that excels in decision-making is crucial for transforming decision-making into a core competitive advantage. In a rapidly changing business environment, quick, informed decisions are what separate leaders from followers. Here's how you can build a cultural flywheel that reinforces strong decision-making at every level.

Thought-Provoking Questions:

1. Consider whether your organization's decision-making processes are efficient and effective. Are decisions being made swiftly, or do bottlenecks slow down progress? Do you regularly conduct after-action reviews of major decisions to assess the effectiveness of

the underlying processes and thinking, in addition to the outcome? Are your processes data-driven, cross-functional, and focused on the Main Thing?

2. Reflect on whether your governance frameworks clearly outline decision rights and responsibilities. Are these structures well-communicated and aligned with the organization's strategic goals, or do they create unnecessary bureaucracy? Evaluate whether the decision-making authority is clearly defined and understood across all levels.

3. Assess whether your organization invests in developing employees' decision-making skills. Do employees have access to the necessary tools, training, and resources to make well-informed decisions?

4. Do your screening and interview processes for new recruits assess the person's fit for a fast, effective decision-making culture?

Turning Thought into Action:

1. Conduct a Thorough Assessment of Decision-Making Capabilities. Begin by evaluating your organization's current decision-making processes and structures. Use surveys and interviews to gather feedback from employees at all levels, and analyze the time taken for decisions to be made and implemented. This assessment will identify gaps and areas for improvement.

2. Establish Strong Governance and Clear Decision-Making Structures. Define decision rights at all levels of the organization, ensuring that employees understand their scope of decision-making authority. Establish a governance framework that supports swift decision-making while maintaining alignment with the organization's strategic goals. Communicate these structures broadly to ensure clarity and consistency.

3. Invest in Talent Development for Decision-Making. Implement training programs focused on critical thinking, problem-solving, and decision-making frameworks. Provide tools and resourc-

es, such as data analytics platforms, to support informed decision-making. Encourage a culture of continuous learning where employees are motivated to improve their decision-making skills through practice and feedback.

4. Ensure Alignment with Organizational Strategy. Regularly communicate the organization's strategic goals to ensure that decision-makers understand how their decisions contribute to these objectives. Use alignment meetings and strategic planning sessions to maintain consistency in decision-making with the organization's long-term objectives.

5. Recruit and Promote for Decision-Making Competence. Integrate decision-making competencies into your recruitment and selection process. Evaluate candidates on their ability to think critically, act decisively, and collaborate effectively. Make decision-making ability a key criterion for promotions and leadership development within the organization.

By focusing on these areas, you can build a culture where decision-making becomes a competitive advantage, driving faster, more effective actions that keep your organization ahead of the competition.

Resources

I have created a set of companion tools that can help you implement the concepts shared in the book. Here is a link to those tools:

Conclusion:

As we've explored in this chapter, decision-making is more than just a process; it's a strategic capability that, when effectively harnessed, can drive competitive advantage and propel an organization forward. By embedding strong governance, developing decision-making talent, and ensuring alignment across the organization, you can transform decision-making from a potential pitfall into a powerful engine for growth.

Ultimately, your company's ability to make decisions better and faster than the competition will define your position in the market. By committing to continuous improvement in decision-making, you not only enhance your organization's efficiency but also create a culture that thrives on clarity, accountability, and action.

Now let's turn our attention to the integration of Decision-Making and Empowerment & Accountability, the building blocks of Velocity.

CLARITY AND GROWTH

Fueling Momentum: How Growth Incentives and Clarity Drive Cultural Velocity

In the Momentum Culture framework, Velocity represents the acceleration of your cultural energy, ensuring that the momentum built through Fusion, and aligned through Vector, is moving at full speed. As we have discussed Velocity is built by creating effective Connections with management through Empowerment & Accountability and the fundamental Capability of Decision Making.

The intersection of these two Factors creates two critical Dynamics in a Momentum Culture. By recognizing and rewarding employees to make decisions indexed to the organization's core strategy, you ensure that you encourage employees to focus on growth initiatives. And when you clearly communicate roles and responsibilities, rights and accountabilities for the decisions within the organization, you provide the clarity employees need to operate with autonomy and speed.

These two essential dynamics, **Encouraging Growth** and **Providing Clarity** are the accelerants that drive your organization to achieve its strategic goals with speed and precision. Encouraging Growth creates the conditions where employees are motivated to stretch their capabilities and pursue excellence, while Providing Clarity ensures that every member of the organization understands their role and the path forward, reducing friction and enhancing focus.

ENCOURAGING GROWTH

Encouraging Growth is vital in propelling an organization's momentum forward by ensuring that employees are rewarded for behaviors that drive desired business outcomes. This approach focuses on creating a culture where growth and excellence are not just encouraged but systematically rewarded.

Key Aspects of Encouraging Growth

Encouraging Growth revolves around three critical aspects: balancing challenges with support, recognizing excellence, and investing in leadership development. The first aspect emphasizes the need to push employees toward ambitious goals while ensuring they have the support needed to achieve them. Leaders must set challenging yet realistic targets, striking a balance that fosters growth without leading to burnout. The second aspect involves offering differential rewards for those who perform beyond expectations, creating a powerful incentive for others to excel. This practice reinforces the organization's commitment to excellence and recognizes individual contributions. Lastly, investing in leadership development ensures that leaders are equipped to guide their teams effectively, aligning their decision-making capabilities with the company's growth objectives.

Importance in a Momentum Culture

In a Momentum Culture, Encouraging Growth plays a crucial role in boosting cultural engagement. When employees are motivated to exceed expectations and are rewarded accordingly, they become more committed to the organization's success. This alignment of individual ambitions with the company's strategic goals creates a unified force that drives the organization forward. Research indicates that organizations prioritizing growth through effective incentives see significant improvements in employee engagement and overall performance.

Momentum Assessment - Encouraging Growth

Our assessment of Encouraging Growth focuses on evaluating how effectively leaders challenge their teams while avoiding unrealistic goals, the fairness of differential rewards for exceptional performance, and the organization's commitment to building leadership capabilities. We examine whether leaders are setting ambitious yet achievable targets that stretch their teams without leading to burnout. Additionally, the assessment looks at how differential rewards are applied to recognize and encourage high performance, ensuring that excellence is rewarded in a way that motivates others. Lastly, we evaluate the organization's investment in leadership development, particularly in enhancing decision-making capabilities, to ensure leaders are equipped to guide their teams toward achieving growth objectives. By understanding these dimensions, we provide insights into how well the organization is fostering a culture of growth and excellence, identifying opportunities to strengthen these practices.

BUILD YOUR CULTURAL FLYWHEEL

1. Set ambitious but realistic goals for your teams, ensuring they are stretched but not overwhelmed. Provide the necessary resources and support to help them achieve these targets.

2. Implement a differential reward system that acknowledges and celebrates employees who consistently perform above expectations, creating an incentive for others to follow suit.

3. Regularly communicate how individual efforts contribute to the company's strategic goals, reinforcing the importance of alignment and shared success in driving the organization forward.

4. Continuously assess the effectiveness of your incentive programs, adjusting as needed to ensure they remain aligned with evolving business strategies and objectives.

By integrating these practices, your organization can create a culture where growth is incentivized at every level, driving sustained momentum and long-term success.

PROVIDING CLARITY

Providing Clarity is a vital component of organizational success, particularly in the context of Velocity, where clear direction is needed to maintain momentum. Clarity involves ensuring that every team member understands their roles, responsibilities, and the expectations placed upon them. It encompasses clear communication, well-defined roles, and structured decision-making processes, all of which are essential for aligning efforts with organizational goals. Without clarity, even the most motivated teams can become misaligned, leading to inefficiencies, missed opportunities and poor decisions.

Key Aspects of Providing Clarity

Providing Clarity is built on three foundational pillars: clear communication of expectations, defined roles and responsibilities, and structured decision-making processes. Clear communication ensures that employees know what is expected of them, reducing uncertainty and empowering them to focus on key objectives. Defined roles and responsibilities prevent overlap and confusion, ensuring that everyone understands their part in the process. Lastly, structured decision-making processes establish who has the authority to make decisions, involve the right stakeholders, and ensure that decisions align with the company's strategic direction. Together, these elements form a cohesive framework that guides the organization toward its goals.

Importance in a Momentum Culture

In a Momentum Culture, Providing Clarity is essential for maintaining focus and direction. Research consistently shows that organizations with clear communication and well-defined roles experience higher levels of employee engagement and productivity[24]. Clarity ensures that everyone is aligned with the organization's goals, reducing friction and enhancing performance. Without it, the energy and motivation of the workforce can be wasted on misaligned efforts, leading to lost oppor-

---

[24] (Ballard, 2024)

tunities and inefficiencies. Clarity, therefore, is not just a component of organizational success but a critical driver of sustained momentum and performance.

Momentum Culture Assessment - Providing Clarity

Our assessment of Providing Clarity focuses on evaluating how effectively leaders communicate expectations, the clarity of roles and responsibilities, and the structure of decision-making processes within the organization. We examine whether leaders provide frequent feedback, ensuring that employees understand their roles and stay on track. The assessment also explores the decision-making process, determining whether the right people are involved and whether there is a clear understanding of decision ownership, particularly in cross-functional decisions. By assessing these areas, we aim to provide a comprehensive view of how well clarity is maintained within the organization, identifying strengths and areas for improvement to support a culture of alignment and efficiency.

BUILD YOUR CULTURAL FLYWHEEL

- Ensure that leaders regularly communicate clear and concise expectations to their teams, offering frequent feedback to keep employees aligned with organizational goals. Create platforms where employees can seek clarification and receive guidance on their roles and responsibilities.

- Establish clear definitions of roles and responsibilities across the organization, ensuring that everyone understands their part in the process and how it aligns with broader organizational objectives. Regularly review and update role definitions to reflect changes in strategy or organizational structure, maintaining alignment and preventing overlaps.

- Encourage a culture of continuous feedback where leaders and employees regularly check in on progress and alignment, ensuring that everyone remains focused on the organization's goals. Use feedback mechanisms to identify areas of misalignment or confusion and address them promptly to maintain clarity and momentum.

- When employees know what is expected of them and understand how their work contributes to the organization's success, they are more likely to be motivated and committed to achieving those goals.

Resources

I have created a set of companion tools that can help you implement the concepts shared in the book. Here is a link to those tools:

FROM ALIGNMENT TO ACCELERATION: HARNESSING THE POWER OF VELOCITY

Incentivizing Growth has shown us the importance of creating a challenging yet supportive environment where employees are motivated to excel. When leaders stretch their teams with clear and realistic goals, backed by appropriate rewards, they create a culture of continuous improvement and high performance.

Providing Clarity, on the other hand, ensures that this drive is not wasted. It emphasizes the importance of clear communication, defined roles, and structured decision-making processes, allowing the organization to move forward with confidence and precision.

Why does the combination of Incentivizing Growth and Providing Clarity increase speed? The answer lies in the powerful synergy between these two elements; growth provides the energy; clarity provides the direction. Together, they form the foundation of Velocity, ensuring that your organization's cultural momentum is not only sustained but accelerated.

This completes the Momentum Assessment Framework. This framework provides a comprehensive picture of a Momentum Culture and a clear opportunity to evaluate your existing culture and identify areas for change and improvement.

The second part of the Framework is a cultural change model, which somewhat unoriginally uses the word MOMENTuM as an acronym to help you remember the steps. If you want an easy to follow, step by step process for driving cultural change in your organization, the next section is designed for you.

III

THE MOMENTuM PROCESS

20

MOMENTuM PROCESS

Building a Cultural Flywheel: How Small Steps Create Big Change

What if we could think of culture as a tangible force, something as real and powerful as a flywheel? A flywheel is a heavy wheel that takes significant effort to set in motion, but once it's spinning, it builds and maintains its momentum with little additional input. This analogy perfectly captures the essence of a Momentum Culture: initially, it may take concentrated effort to establish the desired culture, but once momentum is built, that culture becomes a self-sustaining force that propels the entire organization forward.

The journey to creating a cultural flywheel begins with understanding that every small step, every strategic action, contributes to building momentum. This isn't about grand gestures or sweeping changes overnight. It's about consistent, intentional actions that help you align your culture to the key tenets of the Momentum Culture framework.

In this section of the book, we'll walk you through the seven critical steps of building cultural momentum in your organization. I have organized those tactics into a step-by-step process, using the acronym, MO-MENTu—**Measure, Organize, Map, Establish, Navigate, Transform, and Monitor**—each step contributing to the gradual acceleration of your cultural flywheel.

Whether you are starting from scratch or refining an existing culture, these steps provide a roadmap to ensure your cultural efforts are not just a flash in the pan but a lasting, self-sustaining force.

1. **Measure:** The journey begins with assessing the current state of your organization's culture. Through a combination of qualitative and quantitative methods—such as surveys, interviews, and focus groups—you'll establish a clear baseline. This critical step reveals where your culture stands today, identifying both strengths and areas for improvement, and sets the foundation for all subsequent efforts.

2. **Organize:** Once you've gathered the data, it's time to make sense of it. In this phase, you'll synthesize the information into coherent insights that diagnose your organization's cultural health. By analyzing numerical data, identifying key cultural drivers, and creating a narrative that explains the current state, you transform raw data into actionable insights that guide your next moves.

3. **Map:** With a clear understanding of your current culture, the next step is to map out the desired future state. This involves defining the cultural attributes that will drive your business strategy forward. You'll develop a high-level design that includes new values, leadership styles, and behavioral expectations, ensuring that your culture aligns with and supports your business goals.

4. **Establish:** Establishing new norms is where the rubber meets the road. Here, you'll define the specific mindsets, skills, behaviors, structures, and processes that will embody your desired culture. This step involves setting new standards for recruitment, performance management, and rewards, ensuring that every aspect of your organization reflects and reinforces the culture you aim to build.

5. *Navigate:* Change doesn't happen in a vacuum. In this step, you'll navigate the complexities of rolling out your new culture across the organization. This involves clear communication, consistent reinforcement, and strategic use of cultural symbols and rituals to embed the new norms into everyday operations.

6. **Transform:** Transformation is the culmination of your efforts. This step focuses on leadership, ensuring that those at the top model the desired culture through their actions and decisions. It's about

creating a culture of accountability and empowerment, where leaders and employees alike are committed to living the values and behaviors that define your organization.

7. **Monitor:** Finally, a culture is never static. To maintain the momentum you've built, you must continuously monitor cultural adherence and energy levels across the organization. This involves regular pulse surveys, direct observation, and feedback mechanisms to ensure that the culture remains vibrant and aligned with your business objectives.

As you progress through these steps, remember that building a cultural flywheel is a journey, not a sprint. It's about making thoughtful decisions, taking deliberate actions, and maintaining a long-term perspective. The payoff, however, is immense - a culture that fuels your business momentum.

And for those that have experience in change initiatives, you may be thinking that this process feels quite familiar. That may be true. The research that fuels this book was about understanding the nature of a high-performing culture, not reinventing the process of organizational change itself. But the detail I offer in each step offers a few unique elements that came out of the research and are detailed to help you be successful in your pursuit of cultural momentum. And each section includes insightful stories from organizational leaders that will inspire your approach to culture change. Finally, if the research we quoted in the Introduction is correct, and 70% of culture change initiatives fail, you will want every edge you can find to make sure you land in the other 30%.

In the next chapter, we'll dive deep into the first step: **Measure.** Here, we'll explore how to assess the current state of your culture, setting the stage for all the transformative work to come.

21

MEASURE

You Can't Fix What You Can't See: The Hidden Power of Measuring Culture

In any business, it's easy to spot the tangible problems—falling sales, missed deadlines, or a high turnover rate. But what if the most significant issues lie beneath the surface, in the unmeasured and unseen aspects of your culture? Just like a doctor uses diagnostic tools to uncover hidden health issues, leaders must use cultural assessments to reveal the unseen factors that could be holding their organization back.

The journey to cultural transformation begins with a clear understanding of where you stand today. Measuring your culture provides a baseline starting point from which all change is measured and a roadmap to navigate the complexities of cultural evolution. This step ensures that any actions you take are informed by reality, not assumptions. By collecting both quantitative and qualitative data, you gain insights into what your employees truly think, feel, and experience within your organization.

In this chapter, we'll delve into the critical first step of the MOMEN-TuM process: **Measure.** We will explore how to assess your current cultural state, the importance of involving your leadership team in setting the direction, and the methods you can use to gather meaningful data. With the right tools and approach, you can diagnose cultural strengths and weaknesses, making it possible to target your efforts where they will have the greatest impact.

As we move forward, let's explore the keys to success in this critical step of the MOMENTuM process, ensuring that your cultural measurement efforts are effective, insightful, and actionable.

The Power of Knowing

In the early 2010s, Microsoft found itself at a critical juncture. Under the leadership of Satya Nadella, the company sought to undergo a significant cultural transformation to align with its evolving strategic objectives. This transformation was not merely about changing processes or introducing new products; it was about fundamentally reshaping the way the organization operated, thought, and interacted internally and externally. Central to this transformation was the need to measure and understand the existing culture.

To achieve this, Microsoft implemented a series of comprehensive surveys designed to capture the current state of the organization's culture. These surveys were not one-off events but part of an ongoing feedback loop that allowed leadership to continuously assess the alignment between the company's culture and its strategic goals.

The insights gained from these surveys were eye-opening. For instance, they highlighted a need for greater collaboration and openness within the organization, leading to the introduction of new communication practices and leadership behaviors that fostered a more inclusive and innovative environment.

After implementing the culture changes, Microsoft experienced a remarkable transformation. From 2014 to 2021, the company's market value skyrocketed, increasing by over 600% by the end of the decade. This success story illustrates the profound effect that a well-executed cultural transformation can have on a company's performance.

What Measure Looks Like in Practice

In the **Measure** step of the MOMENTuM process, the focus is on developing a comprehensive understanding of your organization's current cultural landscape. This involves a blend of quantitative and qualitative data collection, each offering a unique lens through which to view the culture.

Quantitative data typically comes from surveys designed to capture employee sentiment across a range of cultural factors. These surveys need to be meticulously crafted to ensure statistical relevance and to allow for meaningful slicing and dicing of the data across different organizational subgroups. The goal is not just to capture the surface-level attitudes but to uncover deeper insights into the cultural drivers that influence employee behavior.

Qualitative data, on the other hand, adds richness to the numerical insights by capturing the stories, symbols, and shared experiences that define the culture. Techniques like one-on-one interviews, focus groups, and site observations are employed to gather this type of data. These methods help to identify the cultural memes that pervade the organization—the ideas and behaviors that are passed from person to person, shaping the way people think and act within the company.

Ultimately, the Measure step in MOMENTuM is about laying the groundwork for change by developing a clear, data-driven understanding of the current cultural state. This step is crucial because it provides the baseline against which progress can be measured, ensuring that the cultural transformation is grounded in reality and tailored to the specific needs of the organization.

BUILD YOUR CULTURAL FLYWHEEL

Key Elements of Measure

- *Clear Objectives:* Define the purpose of the cultural assessment. Establish what you aim to achieve with the data, ensuring alignment with the organization's strategic goals.

- *Balanced Data Collection:* Utilize both quantitative surveys for statistical insights and qualitative methods like interviews and focus groups to capture rich, contextual information.

- *Collaborative Culture Team:* Assemble a diverse, cross-functional team to assist in data gathering and to act as champions for the assessment process, ensuring broad representation across the organization.

Before You Begin the Measure Step

- *What's the Real Purpose?* Beyond setting a baseline, what deeper insights are you seeking? Are you ready to confront potential cultural blind spots that might emerge?

- *How Will You Engage Leadership?* How involved is your leadership team in this assessment? Do they understand their critical role in driving the cultural inquiry?

- *Are You Ready to Listen?* Are you prepared to gather unfiltered feedback from employees? How will you create a safe environment for honest, candid input?

- *What Will Success Look Like?* How will you define success in this assessment? Are you focused on short-term metrics or long-term cultural shifts?

Conclusion

The Measure step in the MOMENTuM process is where the foundation of your cultural transformation is laid. As with any transformation, the insights you gain from this step will guide your next moves, providing clarity on where you stand and where you need to go. Just as with the cultural flywheel analogy, the initial effort in measurement may be significant, but it will create the momentum necessary for lasting impact.

With the data gathered, you're ready to move forward in building a culture that drives performance. The next step, Organize, will take this data and transform it into tangible insights. Let's move forward to learn how to bring order and meaning to the data you've gathered, turning raw information into a powerful blueprint for change.

22

ORGANIZE

Turning Data into Direction: The Power of Organizing Cultural Insights

Collecting cultural data is like gathering puzzle pieces. Each piece— whether it's a survey response, interview snippet, or observation—holds part of the picture. But to truly understand your organization's cultural landscape, those pieces need to be organized into a coherent image that drives strategic action. In the MOMENTuM process, the Organize step is where raw data transforms into actionable insights, setting the stage for informed decision-making and meaningful cultural change.

Once the data is gathered, the challenge becomes how to sift through it, identify patterns, and prioritize findings. This step is crucial because it's easy to become overwhelmed by the volume of information. However, when done correctly, organizing cultural insights not only clarifies the current state of your culture but also highlights the key areas that need attention.

In this chapter, we will explore the essential techniques and tools for effectively organizing your cultural data. We'll discuss how to categorize and analyze both qualitative and quantitative information, ensuring that nothing gets lost in the noise. By the end of this chapter, you'll be equipped to turn data into direction, creating a solid foundation for the next steps in your cultural transformation journey.

The Selfish Meme

In the realm of cultural analysis, the concept of a "meme" extends beyond internet jokes and viral videos. Originally coined by evolutionary biologist Richard Dawkins in his book The Selfish Gene, a meme is an idea, behavior, or style that spreads within a culture, much like genes spread within a biological population. Memes are the building blocks of culture, replicating themselves through imitation and communication.

In an organization, culture can be thought of as a "memeplex," a complex system of interrelated memes that define how people think, act, and interact. Just as in biological evolution, only the fittest memes survive, meaning the ideas and behaviors that resonate most strongly within your organization are the ones that shape its culture. These cultural memes could be anything from the way meetings are conducted to the unspoken rules about work-life balance, and they evolve over time, influencing and reinforcing the overall culture.

The **Organize** step in the MOMENTuM process is about sifting through the data you've gathered to identify these dominant memes. By analyzing both quantitative and qualitative data, you can clarify which memes are currently defining and shaping your culture. This step involves more than just organizing data; it's about understanding the narratives and ideas that are most influential within your organization. By identifying the memes that are driving behavior, you can begin to see where your culture is strong, where it may be misaligned with your strategic goals, and where targeted efforts could create positive change.

Organize Your Data

In the **Organize** step of the MOMENTuM process, the primary focus is on transforming raw data into actionable insights that can guide your cultural transformation. This begins with statistical analysis. You have gathered a tremendous amount of data, but just looking at raw values or averages does not provide an accurate picture. You need to employ advanced statistical analysis to accurately separate signal from noise. Without this level of rigor, you will be basing your investment recommendations on unproven conclusions.

The next step is synthesis, where you combine the quantitative results from surveys with the qualitative insights gathered from interviews and focus groups. This synthesis allows you to see the full picture of your organizational culture, capturing both the broad trends and the nuanced details. Again, anecdotal data is colorful and interesting, but without numerical support, it is more emotional than actionable. A key part of this step is identifying dominant memes within your culture. These are the core ideas, behaviors, and patterns that define how your organization operates today. By understanding these memes, you can determine which aspects of your culture need to be reinforced, adjusted, or completely transformed to align with your strategic goals.

Next, you'll involve cross-functional teams in the review process. Bringing together diverse perspectives ensures that your analysis is comprehensive and reflective of the entire organization, not just a single department or group. This collaborative approach also promotes a sense of ownership among different teams, as they see their input reflected in the analysis.

Once the data is synthesized and reviewed, it's time to prioritize findings. Not all cultural insights are created equal—some will have a more significant impact on your organization's success than others. By prioritizing the most critical findings, you can focus your efforts on the areas that will yield the greatest return.

Overall, the **Organize** step is about turning data into a clear and actionable understanding of your current culture. This understanding is crucial for the next steps in your cultural transformation, ensuring that your actions are grounded in reality and tailored to the specific needs of your organization.

BUILD YOUR CULTURAL FLYWHEEL

Key Elements of Organize

- *Apply Advanced Statistical Analysis:* Use regression analysis to uncover hidden correlations and inform decision-making.

- *Synthesize Data:* Combine quantitative survey results with qualitative insights from interviews and focus groups for a complete cultural picture.

- *Identify Dominant Memes:* Recognize core cultural ideas and behaviors that define the organization's current state.

- *Involve Cross-Functional Teams:* Engage diverse perspectives to ensure a comprehensive and representative analysis.

- *Prioritize Findings:* Focus on the most critical cultural insights that will have the greatest impact on success.

Before You Begin the Organize Step:

- Do You Have the Right Data? Have you collected sufficient qualitative and quantitative data to provide a comprehensive view of your current culture?

- Is Your Team Prepared? Have you assembled a cross-functional team equipped to analyze and interpret the data effectively?

- What Are Your Priorities? Have you determined the criteria for prioritizing cultural elements that will drive the most impactful change?

Conclusion

The **Organize** step in the MOMENTuM process is where the raw data from your cultural assessment begins to take shape, providing clear insights into the state of your organization's culture. By synthesizing qualitative and quantitative insights, involving cross-functional teams, and identifying dominant cultural memes, you set the stage for targeted cultural interventions. This step transforms abstract data into actionable knowledge, allowing you to pinpoint the areas that will have the most significant impact on your organization's journey toward a stronger, more aligned culture.

In the next chapter, we'll explore how to **Map** your path forward, turning insights into a clear vision for your organization's future culture.

23
MAP

Mapping the Path to Cultural Excellence: From Vision to Reality

To achieve any form of excellence, you need a clear, strategic map. This is especially true for organizational culture, where the journey from vision to reality requires precise planning and deliberate actions. The **Map** step in the MOMENTuM process is where your cultural aspirations begin to take tangible form. This is where we assemble all of the elements of the Momentum Culture Framework into a cohesive, integrated vision for your organizational culture.

Mapping your cultural path requires deep reflection and intentional design. Drawing from your strategic objectives, you create a high-level cultural design that aligns with your business goals and sets the tone for every interaction within the organization.

In this chapter, we'll explore how to effectively map out the desired state of your culture, ensuring that every aspect supports your vision and strategy. This process will not only help you articulate the cultural values and behaviors that matter most but will also provide a roadmap for how to instill these elements throughout your organization.

Now that we've set the stage, let's dive into the critical insights and steps you need to succeed in this pivotal phase of cultural transformation. We'll explore how to design a cultural map that doesn't just align with your vision but actively drives your organization toward its most ambitious goals.

Dannon's Culture Map: A Blueprint for Growth

I had an interview with Danielle Garde, the current CHRO of CSW Industrials, and she shared a story from her past that offered an interesting case example for culture mapping. In 2009, Garde was with Danone (Dannon at the time in the U.S.) and the company's European leadership team launched plans for substantial expansion in the American market. However, the existing U.S. culture wasn't aligned with the aggressive growth targets the leadership envisioned. Recognizing that cultural transformation was essential to achieving their ambitious goals, the new leadership team under a new President embarked on a journey to redesign the organizational culture from the ground up.

The team started by envisioning what the culture needed to look like to support the desired business outcomes. They identified key areas that required change, including leadership styles, accountability practices, meeting structures, and even the language used within the organization. This cultural map wasn't just a list of changes; it was a comprehensive design for how the business should operate if it truly expected to double its revenue in just a few years.

To bring this vision to life, the leadership took personal responsibility for the change. The President brought his transformational leadership coach into the business to work with senior leaders as well as to train 400 other leaders to instill a mindset of growth and possibility, build collaboration skills, and reinforce a relentless focus on results. Communication and transparency were also prioritized, ensuring that everyone in the organization knew the goals and their role in achieving them.

The results were nothing short of remarkable. By 2014, Dannon's U.S. unit had markedly increased revenues and became the fastest-growing region within the company. This case study illustrates how mapping out a clear cultural blueprint and aligning it with business objectives can create exponential growth.

Mapping Your Culture: Turning Vision into Reality

The **Map** step of the MOMENTuM process is where you translate the cultural data you've organized into a strategic blueprint for the desired state of your organization's culture. This process begins with envisioning the ideal culture that aligns with your business goals. You'll design a Culture Map, which outlines key factors like recruiting practices, onboarding processes, organizational structure, meeting formats, performance management, rewards and recognition, and the mindsets, skills, and behaviors that will drive your business forward.

The key to success in this step is starting with your strategic goals and working backward to design a culture that will act as the fuel for achieving those objectives. The Map step is about more than just setting aspirations; it's about creating a tangible plan for change, informed by the cultural insights gathered in the earlier steps.

To effectively map your culture, begin by defining the norms, values, and behaviors that align with your strategic vision. Consider what aspects of the current culture need to be preserved, which should be adapted, and what new elements need to be introduced. This map will serve as a guiding document for the entire organization, providing clarity on the cultural shifts required to achieve your business goals.

BUILD YOUR CULTURAL FLYWHEEL

Key Elements of Map

- *Envision the Ideal Culture:* Define the cultural attributes that align with your strategic objectives.
- *Design the Cultural Map:* Outline key factors like recruiting, onboarding, structure, meetings, performance management, rewards, and behaviors.
- *Align Culture with Strategy:* Ensure the cultural design supports the business goals and drives performance.

- *Preserve, Adapt, Introduce:* Identify which elements of the current culture should be kept, modified, or newly introduced.

Before You Begin the Map Step

- *Is Your Vision Clear?* Have you clearly defined the strategic goals that your culture needs to support? Are these goals well-communicated across the organization?

- *Do You Understand the Current State?* Have you fully analyzed the cultural insights gathered in the previous steps to identify what needs to change?

- *Are You Ready to Engage Stakeholders?* How will you involve key stakeholders in the mapping process to ensure buy-in and alignment with the strategic vision?

- *What Are Your Priorities?* Which cultural elements are most critical to align with your business goals, and which can be addressed later?

- *Do You Have the Tools?* Are you equipped with the right frameworks, models, and methodologies to effectively design and communicate the desired culture?

Conclusion

The **Map** step in the MOMENTuM process is where vision meets strategy. It's the stage where you take the insights gathered about your current culture and align them with your organization's strategic goals to design a future state that drives success. By thoughtfully mapping out this desired culture, you lay the groundwork for transformative change that is both intentional and actionable.

As we move into the next phase, **Establish**, you'll see how this cultural map becomes a living blueprint—guiding the creation of new norms, behaviors, and practices that will sustain the momentum of your organizational transformation. Let's delve into how to bring this cultural vision to life, ensuring that your organization not only embraces change but thrives in it.

24

ESTABLISH

The Blueprint for Success: Establishing Cultural Norms That Drive Performance

Establishing new cultural norms is like adding depth and color to your cultural vision. These norms, when aligned with your strategic goals, become the foundation upon which a high-performing culture is built. This step in the MOMENTuM process is about defining and embedding the mindsets, skills, and behaviors that will propel your organization forward.

As we move through this chapter, we'll explore how to establish these norms in a way that accelerates your business objectives. We'll look at how to identify and cultivate the key behaviors that align with success, how to recruit and develop talent that fits your cultural vision, and how to create new rituals and metrics that reinforce the desired state.

Aligning Culture with Business Outcomes

I had an interview with the leader of a large, regional construction company based in Western Pennsylvania. They consistently work to align its culture with the desired business outcome of high-quality work. Central to this alignment was the role of the Superintendent, a position that required high-quality individuals who needed to be omnipresent on the job to achieve the excellent project outcomes they promised. Unlike most companies that treat this role as a salaried position, they decided to make it an hourly role - not to demean the position but to incentivize Superintendents to be present on-site throughout the project.

This approach means paying out expensive overtime regularly, but the company views it as a worthwhile investment. The rationale is simple: by aligning the compensation structure with the desired outcome of constant supervision and presence, the company ensures that the individuals in these key roles are happy, well-compensated, and motivated to perform their best. The result is a consistent level of excellence in the quality of work, with Superintendents fully engaged and invested in their projects. This case illustrates how aligning work structures, as well as rewards and recognition, with desired cultural outcomes, can drive organizational success and create a culture that supports business goals.

Establishing New Norms: A Blueprint for Cultural Alignment

Establishing new cultural norms is where strategy meets execution, transforming abstract ideals into tangible behaviors and practices that define your organization's culture. This step is crucial as it determines how well your organization can align its daily operations with its strategic goals. By defining the mindsets, skills, and behaviors that drive success, creating bold and memorable rules, and aligning compensation with desired outcomes, you ensure that the culture you envision becomes the culture that drives performance.

Establishing new norms requires a multifaceted approach, starting with a clear understanding of the leadership competencies and behaviors that align with your desired culture. It involves redefining recruitment practices to attract and retain individuals who embody these cultural values and integrating these norms into every aspect of your organization, from performance management to daily rituals.

One of the most critical aspects of establishing new norms is the alignment of rewards and recognition with the desired cultural outcomes. By engineering work structures that support these norms and compensating employees in ways that reinforce them, you create a powerful incentive system that drives the right behaviors and ensures long-term cultural sustainability.

The success of this step hinges on the clarity and boldness of the rules and expectations you set. Clear, memorable, and impactful rules ensure that the desired behaviors are encountered daily and remain at the forefront of employees' minds. This not only drives consistency but also builds momentum as these behaviors become ingrained in the organizational fabric.

BUILD YOUR CULTURAL FLYWHEEL

Key Elements of Establish

- *Define Critical Mindsets and Behaviors:* Establish the mindsets, skills, and behaviors essential for organizational success.

- *Recruitment Aligned with Culture:* Implement hiring practices that prioritize cultural fit over experience or pedigree.

- *Create Bold and Clear Rules:* Establish memorable rules that reinforce desired behaviors and are encountered daily.

- *Align Rewards with Desired Outcomes:* Design compensation and recognition systems that support and reinforce the new cultural norms.

- *Engineering Work Structures:* Ensure organizational structures and processes are designed to facilitate and sustain the desired culture.

Before You Begin the Establish Step:

- *What Cultural Norms Need Redefining?* Are there existing behaviors or practices that conflict with your desired culture? Consider how these might be reengineered to align with your new objectives.

- *How Will You Acquire and Retain Momentum Talent?* Have you defined the values and skills that are critical for your culture? What processes will you implement to ensure you attract and retain individuals who embody these traits?

- *Is Your Leadership Aligned with the New Norms?* Have you clearly communicated the expectations for leadership behavior? How will you ensure leaders model the cultural changes you wish to implement?

Conclusion

The **Establish** step is where the foundation of your cultural transformation becomes real, turning insights into action. By focusing on the key mindsets, skills, and behaviors that align with your vision, you're not only setting new expectations but also ensuring that every aspect of the organization, from recruiting to rewards, is geared towards success.

With these new elements in place, the momentum you've generated sets the stage for the next critical step: **Navigate.** This is where you will guide your organization through the complexities of change, ensuring that your newly established norms are fully integrated and embraced across the board.

25
NAVIGATE

From Strategy to Execution: Navigating Cultural Change

Navigating cultural change demands meticulous execution to bridge the gap between intention and impact. Cultural transformation is like setting a course on a vast ocean—having a map is essential, but it's the navigator's skill that ensures the ship reaches its destination. This chapter explores the critical steps and considerations for successfully deploying a new culture within your organization, ensuring that the desired changes not only take root but flourish, driving your organization towards its strategic goals.

The Broken Windows Theory

The head of talent for a prominent manufacturer in the aerospace sector shared a prime example of how cultural misalignment can have significant consequences. At any manufacturing company, maintaining a mature safety culture is crucial for ensuring consistent production yield, employee safety, and overall quality. However, despite the company's verbal commitment to safety, there was a glaring disconnect between stated values and day-to-day operations.

For instance, during the winter months, the facility would frequently experience snowfall, creating hazardous conditions. One would expect a company committed to safety to ensure that the parking lots were clear of ice, and safer than the surrounding roads. Yet, this was often not the case. The parking lot was typically more dangerous than the roads managed by local authorities, a visible sign of the company's failure to observably demonstrate its safety culture.

This situation can be understood through the lens of the Broken Windows Theory, a criminological theory developed by James Q. Wilson and George L. Kelling in 1982[25]. The theory posits that visible signs of disorder and neglect, such as broken windows, can lead to an increase in crime and antisocial behavior. The idea is that when minor issues are left unaddressed, it sends a signal that disorder is tolerated, leading to more significant problems.

At this company, the unaddressed safety hazards acted like "broken windows." Employees saw that the company's stated commitment to safety was not reflected in their actions, leading to a decline in trust and a sense of disconnection from the organizational values. Just as broken windows can lead to an increase in crime, these visible inconsistencies eroded the culture, undermining the company's efforts to foster a strong, safety-first environment, resulting in a below standard level of safety that resulted in meaningful impact to employee health outcomes.

The lesson here is clear: in any cultural transformation, small visible signals can have an outsized impact. For this manufacturer, this meant that their failure to maintain safety standards in the small things had a ripple effect, creating a culture where the stated values were not taken seriously, leading to disastrous outcomes for workers.

This case underscores the importance of coherence between what an organization says and what it does. For cultural change to take root, there must be alignment between words and actions, with visible symbols and behaviors reinforcing the desired culture at every level.

Navigating the Cultural Transformation Process

In the **Navigate** step of the MOMENTuM process, the focus shifts from planning to execution—transforming the carefully laid out strategies into concrete actions that will embed the desired culture throughout the organization. This phase is where the real work begins, as leaders must guide their teams through the complexities of change, ensuring

[25] (Wilson & Kelling, 1982)

that the new cultural norms are not just understood but fully integrated into daily operations.

One of the first tasks in this step is to determine how the cultural change will be launched within the organization. Will it be a top-down directive from leadership, or will it emerge as a grassroots movement with broad employee involvement? This decision sets the tone for the entire change initiative. If the approach is too rigidly controlled from the top, it may fail to resonate with employees, leading to resistance or apathy. On the other hand, if it's too loosely defined, it might lack the cohesion needed to drive consistent change.

Communication is another critical element of this phase. The organization needs a comprehensive communication strategy that not only informs employees about the new cultural direction but also inspires them to embrace it. This includes crafting clear, compelling messages that resonate across different levels of the organization, ensuring that everyone from senior leaders to frontline employees understands and supports the new cultural vision.

A practical way to facilitate this communication is by "meme-ifying" the cultural messages—creating simple, repeatable, and engaging stories or slogans that can be easily spread and remembered. This strategy was effectively employed by Invitrogen, where Belinda Hyde shared their campaign to create alignment between Vision and Strategy. By treating the internal communication of culture change almost like an advertising campaign, with a focus on branding and ubiquity, Invitrogen was able to ensure that the new cultural messages permeated every level of the organization.

In addition to communication, the formation of a Culture Diffusion Team can be especially effective. This cross-functional team acts as the driving force behind the cultural shift, helping to spread the new norms and behaviors throughout the organization. They play the role of culture champions, engaging with their peers, addressing concerns, and fostering a sense of ownership and involvement in the change process.

Visible symbols and actions also play a significant role in navigating cultural change. Employees are more likely to believe in the new culture if they see it reflected in the physical environment, leadership behaviors, and day-to-day operations. Leadership must consistently demonstrate the behaviors they wish to see in their teams, as any disconnect between words and actions can quickly erode trust and undermine the entire initiative.

Navigating cultural change requires a combination of clear communication, strong leadership, and a deep understanding of the organization's current and desired states. By carefully guiding the deployment of new cultural norms, leaders can ensure that the change is not just a temporary shift but a lasting transformation that propels the organization forward.

BUILD YOUR CULTURAL FLYWHEEL

Key Elements of Navigate

- *Launch Strategy:* Decide how the cultural change will be initiated—whether through top-down leadership or grassroots involvement—and align this approach with your organizational dynamics.

- *Comprehensive Communication:* Develop and implement a strategic communication plan that clearly conveys the cultural vision, using memorable and engaging messages to ensure widespread understanding and adoption.

- *Culture Diffusion Team:* Establish a cross-functional team to champion and drive cultural change, ensuring that the new norms are embraced and spread throughout the organization.

- *Visible Symbols and Actions:* Ensure that the new culture is consistently demonstrated through leadership behaviors, environmental cues, and daily operations to build trust and reinforce the change.
- *Continuous Engagement:* Regularly assess and adjust the approach as needed, maintaining momentum and addressing any resistance or challenges that arise during the cultural transition.

Before You Begin Navigate:

1. *Is Your Communication Strategy Clear?* Have you defined how you will communicate the cultural changes across different levels of the organization? Is there a plan to make the messaging consistent and impactful?

2. *Who Will Lead the Cultural Movement?* Have you identified and empowered a cross-functional team that will champion the new culture throughout the organization?

3. *Are Visible Actions Aligned with the New Culture?* How will you ensure that the leadership and environment visibly reflect the cultural changes you want to implement?

4. *What Will You Do When Resistance Arises?* Do you have a plan to address pushbacks and maintain momentum when challenges to the cultural change emerge?

Conclusion

Navigating cultural change is where strategy meets reality. This step is about transforming your cultural vision into actionable steps, ensuring that your organization's behaviors and beliefs align with your strategic goals. As you've seen, the success of this phase relies heavily on consistent communication, visible leadership, and the engagement of every level of your organization. It's not enough to declare a new culture—you must live it, demonstrate it, and ensure that it permeates every aspect of the organization.

As you move into the next step, **Transform**, you'll focus on empowering leaders to model the desired culture and drive the change forward.

TRANSFORM

Walking the Talk: Transforming Culture Through Leadership

Cultural transformation is one of the most challenging endeavors an organization can undertake. It's not enough to outline a vision or articulate new values; for a culture to truly transform, it requires leaders to lead by example. The concept of "walking the talk" is critical because employees are far more likely to adopt new behaviors when they see them modeled consistently by their leaders. When leaders visibly and authentically embody the desired cultural attributes, they send a powerful message that resonates across the organization.

This chapter delves into how leadership actions—far more than words—can drive true cultural transformation. By focusing on how leaders spend their time, allocate resources, and make decisions, we explore the ways in which these actions become the visible proof of a leader's commitment to the desired culture.

We'll also examine how egalitarian leadership can reinforce this transformation. Leaders must not only act as the architects of cultural change but also as their most ardent supporters and participants. When leaders "walk the talk", they pave the way for others to follow, making the vision of a transformed culture a living reality.

Now, let's delve into the key insights that will guide successful cultural transformation through leadership. HP offers a couple of powerful anecdotes that underscore how culture is transformed.

Transforming Together: The HP 9-Day Fortnight

In the early 1970s, Hewlett-Packard (HP) faced a severe economic down-turn that threatened jobs and stability. Rather than resorting to layoffs, HP leadership chose a different path—a radical work schedule known as the 9-Day Fortnight[26]. This schedule allowed employees to work nine days over two weeks instead of the typical ten, effectively cutting their hours by 10% while still preserving their jobs.

This move was more than a cost-saving measure; it was a powerful state-ment of solidarity. By opting for a shared sacrifice, HP's leaders demon-strated that they valued their employees' well-being and were commit-ted to weathering the storm together. This decision reinforced the idea that in a strong organizational culture, everyone is in it together, and leadership is about standing shoulder-to-shoulder with the team, not just dictating from above.

The 9-Day Fortnight became a symbol of HP's commitment to its peo-ple, proving that transformative leadership is about more than just making tough decisions—it's about making the right ones, even when they require shared sacrifices. This approach not only preserved jobs but also strengthened trust and loyalty within the organization, setting a lasting example of what it means to truly lead by example in times of crisis. This egalitarian feeling is a hallmark of Momentum Culture.

Growing Leaders to Transform Culture: The Talent Culture at HP

But it is just as important that workers feel that they are continually growing. When Susan Burnett was the VP of Organizational Effective-ness at HP, she recognized that HP's way of growing leadership talent was essential to sustaining a strong, innovative culture. Having spent the first part of her career at HP in multiple businesses, in the market-ing, sales enablement, and HR functions, she benefitted from managers who exposed her to different opportunities. The best managers pushed

---

[26] (Hewlett Packard, n.d.)

her to leave her function and get cross-functional experience and challenged her with new roles that were out of her comfort zone. Burnett shared,

> *"Growing great leaders was part of every manager's objective, and since Bill Hewlett and Dave Packard invented MBO, every employee knew those objectives were more than an annual exercise at HP. That also meant we were evaluated by our ability to build the next generation of talent. You couldn't hoard talent at HP; that would be counter to the culture."*

One of her challenges was to institute some formal succession processes without breaking the informal system of internal movement that had worked so well in the past. But HP was getting very big, very global and very complex, and she needed to create something that was familiar to employees so it would stick. So, she leaned on the concept of HP's Vintage Chart, traditionally used to track revenue from product innovation, and created the concept of a Talent Vintage Chart. This new chart illustrated how leaders within HP were developed and advanced to lead other parts of the business.

> *"For the first time, we were codifying who our high potential leaders were, tracking them and providing them with the skills and experiences they needed to reach executive levels."*

By showcasing the progression of leaders in executive reviews, HP not only recognized and celebrated those who cultivated talent but also made it clear that growing people from within was still a core organizational value. This practice didn't just track progress; it preserved the company's culture, continuing to embed leadership development into the fabric of HP's identity. The Talent Vintage Chart became a powerful symbol of HP's commitment to internal growth, ensuring that leadership was continuously nurtured from within, aligned with the company's long-term vision, and reflective of the cultural values HP sought to promote.

EXECUTING A CULTURE TRANSFORMATION THROUGH LEADERSHIP

In the Transform step of the MOMENTuM process, the focus is on turning cultural aspirations into reality through the deliberate actions of leaders. At the heart of this transformation is the idea that leadership is not about what you say but what you do. Leaders set the tone for the entire organization; their behaviors, priorities, and decisions become the blueprint for the culture. As the saying goes, "We are what we do," and this becomes especially relevant when leaders are the primary drivers of cultural change. Employees closely observe where leaders spend their time and resources, interpreting these actions as clear indicators of what truly matters in the organization. A leader once distilled this for me very eloquently,

> *"If you want to know what I truly stand for, you only need to look at two things - my calendar and my credit card statement. Because they show where I spend my time and what I spend money on. The rest is just lip service."*

So, to transform culture, leaders must be intentional in allocating time and resources in ways in accordance with the organization's *"Main Thing"*.

Coaching, too, plays a pivotal role in transforming culture. By embedding coaching into the leadership approach, organizations can create an environment where employees feel supported in their personal and professional growth. Coaching fosters two-way communication, builds trust, and empowers employees to take ownership of their development. This bi-directional benefit is highlighted in a quote by engineer and author, Robert Heinlein,

"When one teaches, two learn."

Coaching takes this idea a step further, and I have adapted this quote to,

"When one coaches, two grow."

The philosophy speaks to the fact that coaching benefits both the coach and the coachee, amplifying the cultural transformation across the organization. This integration strengthens the overall culture, ensuring that the desired behaviors and mindsets are consistently reinforced in all directions.

Effective communication is essential to sustain this transformation. Leaders must use every opportunity to reinforce the cultural vision, whether through formal channels like meetings and newsletters or informal ones like one-on-one conversations. Clear, consistent communication ensures that the cultural message is understood and embraced at all levels of the organization. This communication, coupled with aligned rewards and recognition systems, helps to embed the new culture deeply within the organization.

Lastly, addressing cultural violations is crucial for maintaining the integrity of the transformation. Leaders must be prepared to act when behaviors deviate from the desired culture, sending a clear message that the organization is serious about the cultural shift. By addressing these issues promptly, leaders can prevent erosion of the new norms and reinforce the organization's commitment to cultural transformation.

BUILD YOUR CULTURAL FLYWHEEL

Key Elements of Transform:

- *Leadership Modeling:* Leaders must consistently demonstrate the desired cultural behaviors through their actions and decisions.

- *Talent Development:* Invest in growing people from within to reinforce the cultural transformation and drive continuous improvement.

- *Coaching Integration:* Embed coaching into the leadership approach to foster growth, trust, and alignment with the cultural vision.

- *Leadership Communication:* Use clear and consistent communication to reinforce the cultural vision at all levels of the organization.

- *Addressing Cultural Violations:* Promptly address behaviors that deviate from the desired culture to maintain integrity and commitment to the transformation.

Before You Begin the Transform Step:

- *Are Your Leaders Ready to Model the Desired Culture?* Have you assessed whether your leadership team is prepared to consistently demonstrate the behaviors and values of the new culture? What changes in mindset or behavior might they need to embrace?

- *Is Talent Development a Priority?* How will you ensure that growing talent from within is recognized and rewarded? What systems are in place to track and celebrate these achievements?

- *Is Coaching Embedded in Your Leadership Approach?* Do your leaders have the skills and resources to coach their teams effectively? How will you support them in becoming coaches who can drive cultural transformation?

Conclusion

The **Transform** step in the MOMENTuM process is where the vision for your organizational culture begins to take tangible form. By focusing on leadership modeling, talent development, and embedding a coaching culture, you set the stage for a profound and lasting cultural shift. Leaders who exemplify the desired culture through their actions become powerful catalysts for change, inspiring others to follow suit. As talent grows within the organization, it reinforces the cultural norms that drive success, while coaching ensures that everyone is aligned and continuously evolving.

As you complete the **Transform** step, your organization will be on the brink of a fully integrated cultural change. The next step, **Monitor**, will ensure that these transformations are sustained over time.

27

MONITOR

Keeping Your Finger on the Pulse: How to Monitor and Sustain Cultural Momentum

In the journey of cultural transformation, achieving change is just the beginning. The real challenge lies in sustaining that change and ensuring that the newly established culture continues to thrive. Just as a doctor monitors a patient's vital signs to ensure ongoing health, leaders must keep a vigilant eye on the cultural pulse of their organizations. Monitoring is about being watchful for subtle shifts in organizational energy, ensuring adherence to new norms, and catching signs of complacency before they take root. This chapter explores the essential tools and strategies for keeping your finger on the pulse of your organization, ensuring that the momentum you've built continues to drive your culture and business forward.

Understanding Cultural Maturity: Large Regional Construction Company

Cultural maturity within an organization can be understood through a continuum that ranges from compliance-driven behavior to a culture fully embraced and driven by the employees. At Level 1, which I refer to as Compliance, culture is largely defined by adherence to rules and guidelines established by the organization. This stage is characterized by a focus on compliance, where behaviors are enforced through policies and procedures. While necessary, a culture at this level often lacks the engagement and deeper commitment needed for long-term success.

Progressing to Level 2, Leader-Led, the culture becomes leader driven. Employees begin to accept and internalize the culture, but leadership is still the primary driver of shaping and reinforcing cultural norms. This level of maturity sees stronger alignment with the organization's goals, but it still relies heavily on active leadership to sustain it.

The highest level, Level 3, which I refer to as Interdependence, represents a culture that is not only accepted by employees but is also driven by them. At this stage, the culture is characterized by interdependence, trust, and empowerment. Employees at all levels feel a deep sense of ownership over the culture, and it becomes self-sustaining, with a declining need for top-down enforcement. This is the ideal state of cultural maturity, where the culture is most resilient and aligned with the organization's mission and values.

Our case example regional construction company exemplifies a Level 3 culture. With a history spanning nearly a century, they have cultivated a culture of pride and professionalism underpinned by strong values of trust and empowerment. This culture has become deeply ingrained, to the point where the company now employs third-generation family members, highlighting the enduring strength of its foundation.

However, reaching this pinnacle of cultural maturity is only part of the challenge. The leader of the company emphasizes that the true test lies in maintaining this culture. Even in a Level 3 culture, there is a risk of complacency, where the interdependence and trust that hold the culture together can be disrupted by a few misaligned individuals or by a lack of ongoing vigilance.

Their approach to sustaining their culture involves continuous monitoring and a proactive stance against complacency. Leaders are deeply committed to keeping their culture strong, not just by enforcing standards but by actively engaging with employees to ensure that the company's core values remain at the forefront of daily operations. They recognize that cultural maturity is a dynamic process that requires constant attention and nurturing.

Through vigilant monitoring—whether by direct observation, regular feedback, or maintaining open lines of communication—the company ensures that their culture remains vibrant and aligned with their values. This dedication to monitoring and reinforcing their culture is a critical factor in their long-term success, demonstrating that even the most mature cultures require ongoing care to prevent them from slipping back into lower levels of maturity.

Learning Culture by Being Present: HP

Understanding and nurturing an organization's culture can't be accomplished solely through surveys or reports. While these tools provide valuable insights, they only offer a snapshot of the broader picture. To truly grasp the pulse of a company's culture, senior leaders must engage directly with employees on the ground, experiencing the culture firsthand and observing how it manifests in daily interactions.

Direct observation is critical because culture is lived and experienced in the day-to-day moments that define the organization. These are the interactions in meetings, the decisions made under pressure, and the subtle behaviors that reinforce—or undermine—the desired cultural norms. Leaders who rely only on surveys risk missing these nuances, which can lead to blind spots in understanding and steering the culture effectively.

One of the simplest, but perhaps the most successful methodologies for embedding this approach into leadership practices is Management by Walking Around (MBWA), popularized by Hewlett-Packard (HP). MBWA is a hands-on, proactive management style where leaders regularly walk through their workspaces, engaging with employees directly. This approach enables leaders to observe the actual work environment, address concerns in real-time, and demonstrate their commitment to the organization's values.

Bill Hewlett and Dave Packard, the founders of HP, championed MBWA to stay connected with their workforce and maintain a strong, cohesive culture. They believed that being visible and accessible to employees helped bridge the gap between management and the frontline, fostering a sense of belonging and mutual respect.

In practice, MBWA involved leaders spending as much time as possible on the manufacturing floor, interacting with employees to understand their challenges, gauge morale, and ensure that the culture they wanted to cultivate was being lived out daily. Hewlett and Packard demonstrated how they valued employees through their actions, making personal connections and building trust across the organization.

This practice not only made HP's leadership more visible but also created a feedback loop where cultural issues could be identified and addressed before they escalated. The personal engagement fostered by MBWA helped HP maintain a consistent and aligned culture, even as the company grew.

In today's hybrid and remote work environments, replicating MBWA poses new challenges. However, the underlying principle remains the same: leaders must find ways to connect directly with employees, whether through virtual check-ins, scheduled site visits, or other creative means. The key is to ensure that leaders stay engaged and connected, continuously monitoring the cultural pulse to guide the organization effectively. This is one element that senior leaders cannot delegate to proxies.

The Value of Comparative Insight: Aires

While direct observation within a single site can reveal much about an organization's culture, the true depth of understanding often comes from comparing these insights across different locations. This is where executive field visits become indispensable. Leaders who spend time in various offices or facilities can discern subtle differences in how the company's culture is being lived out—or not—in different areas.

Joleen Lauffer, President of Aires, a global mobility services firm, exemplifies this approach. Rather than relying solely on virtual communication or periodic reports, Lauffer makes it a point to visit all her company's global offices regularly. During these visits, she doesn't just speak to employees in formal settings; she observes how work is conducted, how teams interact, and how aligned each office is with the company's overarching cultural goals.

This method allows Lauffer to compare the cultural atmosphere from one location to the next, identifying unique pockets of culture that may exist. These comparisons are invaluable; they help uncover whether cultural inconsistencies exist between sites, enabling leadership to address disparities and ensure a unified organizational culture. The insights gathered during these visits inform strategic decisions, helping to fine-tune leadership approaches and align practices across the company.

By engaging in executive field visits, leaders can avoid the pitfalls of complacency, ensuring that their organization's culture remains vibrant, consistent, and aligned with its strategic objectives. This hands-on approach reinforces the importance of visibility and engagement, demonstrating that the leadership is committed to nurturing and sustaining the desired culture at every level of the organization.

Monitoring Your Culture

To effectively monitor and maintain the health of an organization's culture, leaders must take a proactive and hands-on approach. The first step is to establish cultural benchmarks by clearly defining the key behaviors, values, and outcomes that reflect the desired cultural state. These benchmarks serve as a foundation for all monitoring activities.

Next, regular assessments should be implemented using a combination of qualitative and quantitative methods. Pulse surveys, focus groups, and direct observations provide insights into employee sentiment and how well the culture is being lived within the organization. However, these assessments should not be limited to written or digital reports. Leaders must engage in direct observation—physically or virtually—to experience firsthand the daily manifestations of the company culture.

For organizations with multiple locations, executive field visits play a crucial role. By visiting various sites, leaders can compare cultural adherence across different locations, identifying discrepancies and areas that may need reinforcement. This approach not only helps in understanding the unique subcultures within different pockets of the company but also ensures that the desired culture is consistently applied across the organization.

Monitoring energy levels within the organization is also vital. Pulse surveys and manager feedback help gauge the overall engagement and energy levels of teams, allowing for early detection of cultural fatigue or misalignment. Leadership modeling is another critical aspect; leaders must consistently demonstrate the desired cultural behaviors, as their actions set the tone for the rest of the organization.

Finally, creating feedback loops ensures that the monitoring process remains dynamic and responsive. Employees should have a platform to voice concerns or suggestions regarding the culture, which keeps the monitoring process flexible and adaptable to changes. By regularly reviewing findings and making necessary adjustments, leaders can sustain a healthy and aligned organizational culture.

BUILD YOUR CULTURAL FLYWHEEL

Key Elements of Monitor

- *Establish Cultural Benchmarks:* Define clear cultural goals and desired outcomes.

- *Implement Regular Assessments:* Use pulse surveys, focus groups, and direct observations.

- *Engage in Direct Observation:* Spend time with employees to see the culture firsthand.
- *Leverage Executive Field Visits:* Compare cultural adherence across different locations.
- *Monitor Energy Levels:* Use pulse surveys and feedback to gauge engagement.
- *Ensure Leadership Modeling:* Leaders must consistently demonstrate desired behaviors.
- *Create Feedback Loops:* Allow for continuous feedback and make necessary adjustments.

Before You Begin the Monitor Step

- Are senior leaders committed to consistently modeling the desired culture? Do they understand how their actions will be scrutinized as a benchmark for cultural adherence?
- What specific strategies will you implement to ensure that cultural vigilance is maintained over time, preventing complacency and the erosion of standards as initial enthusiasm wanes?
- Have you established clear, real-time feedback channels that allow for the prompt identification and correction of cultural drift or non-compliance?
- Are the metrics you've chosen truly reflective of the cultural behaviors you want to reinforce? Do they allow for regular, accurate monitoring?
- Do you have a plan in place for how to address issues that arise from your direct observations and assessments? How will you ensure swift and effective corrective actions?

Conclusion

The journey of cultural transformation doesn't end with the deployment of new norms and practices—it's an ongoing process that requires continuous vigilance. Monitoring is critical to maintaining the cultural changes you've worked so hard to implement. By regularly assessing cultural adherence and organizational energy, you ensure that the culture remains vibrant, aligned with your vision, and resistant to complacency.

The three-tiered model of cultural maturity—from compliance to interdependence—serves as a guide for understanding where your organization stands and where it might need reinforcement. But even in mature states, Momentum Cultures require constant vigilance to prevent cultural entropy.

In the next chapter, we'll revisit the entire MOMENTuM process, reflecting on how each step interconnects to create a cohesive framework for cultural transformation. Together, we'll explore how these steps combine to drive sustainable, long-term change in your organization, ensuring that the cultural flywheel you've set in motion continues to turn, generating positive results for years to come.

28 MOMENTUM CYCLE

Culture in Motion: The Perpetual Cycle of Alignment and Energy

Culture is not a static force; it's a living, breathing ecosystem that evolves constantly, much like the organizations it inhabits. As your business grows, shifts, and faces new challenges, so too does your culture. But unlike strategy, which often follows a clear trajectory, culture requires ongoing nurturing, monitoring, and alignment. Think of it as a cycle in perpetual motion—never truly complete, either gaining or losing Momentum, and requiring continuous attention to maintain its vibrancy.

In this chapter, we'll explore the MOMENTuM process as a dynamic, ongoing cycle that keeps your organizational culture aligned with your strategic goals. We'll delve into the natural tendencies of cultures to drift towards entropy and how conscious effort is required to keep them healthy and aligned. You'll also discover why understanding the culture you want is critical to guiding it effectively and how the integration of culture and strategy creates a powerful synergy that drives business results. This chapter will highlight the importance of viewing culture not as a box to check off but as a living ecosystem that needs to be tended to with the same care and attention as any other critical aspect of your business.

The Natural Drift Towards Entropy

Throughout this book, we have explored the effect of entropy on corporate culture. By acknowledging the natural tendency towards entropy, you can take proactive steps to keep your culture aligned with your strategic goals, ensuring that it remains a source of energy and strength rather than a liability.

The Power of a Clear Cultural Vision

Understanding that culture naturally drifts towards entropy underscores the importance of having a clear and compelling vision of the culture you want to build. Without this vision, efforts to guide or change culture are aimless and ineffective. Leaders must not only know the culture they want but also articulate it clearly, ensuring that every member of the organization understands what is expected and why it matters.

By knowing the culture you want, and using the MOMENTuM Process as your guide, you can transform your organization into a cohesive, high-performing entity that's fully aligned with your strategic ambitions.

Integrating Culture and Strategy: A Symbiotic Relationship

Culture and strategy are not separate entities—they are two sides of the same coin, each influencing and reinforcing the other. A well-crafted strategy without an aligned culture is like a beautifully designed ship without a capable crew; it may look promising, but it won't get far. Conversely, a strong culture without a clear strategy is directionless, lacking the focus needed to achieve meaningful results.

Integration of culture and strategy is a cornerstone of Momentum Culture. The culture you build should be intentionally designed to push your strategy forward, creating a dynamic environment where every action, decision, and behavior is aligned with your strategic goals. This alignment ensures that your culture becomes a powerful enabler of your strategy, rather than a passive backdrop.

Leaders who overlook this integration, treating culture and strategy as separate endeavors, risk creating a disconnect that can lead to inefficiencies, misaligned priorities, and ultimately, failure to achieve desired outcomes. When culture and strategy are in harmony, however, they create a self-reinforcing cycle that propels the organization toward success.

The MOMENTuM Culture Framework is specifically designed to help leaders achieve this integration. By using the framework to align cultural initiatives with strategic objectives, organizations can create a cohesive force that drives performance, innovation, and sustainable growth.

The Living Ecosystem: Embracing Culture as a Perpetual Cycle

Culture is not static; it's a living, breathing ecosystem that evolves and shifts over time. Just as in any ecosystem, various elements interact with one another, influencing the overall health and direction of the culture. This dynamic nature means that cultural transformation is not a one-time project with a clear endpoint—it's a perpetual cycle that requires ongoing attention and adaptation.

By viewing culture as a perpetual cycle rather than a finite project, leaders can foster a resilient, adaptive organization. This mindset allows you to keep the cultural flywheel spinning, ensuring that the energy, alignment, and momentum you've worked so hard to build continue to propel your organization toward long-term success. The MOMENTuM process becomes not just a roadmap for transformation but a guide for sustaining a vibrant, high-performing culture over time.

Resources

I have created a set of companion tools that can help you implement the concepts shared in the book. Here is a link to those tools:

Conclusion

As we close this exploration of the MOMENTuM process, it's essential to understand that cultivating a high-performing organizational culture is not a one-time event but an ongoing journey. The process is built on four core insights:

First, cultural entropy reminds us that without intentional effort, alignment and energy naturally decline, making continuous focus imperative. Second, having a clear vision of the desired culture is crucial to effectively guide or transform the current state. Third, integrating culture with strategy ensures that your cultural efforts are not just abstract ideals but actively drive your business forward. Finally, the understanding that culture is a living ecosystem reinforces the need for ongoing monitoring and adjustment, recognizing that the MOMENTuM process is a perpetual cycle, not a linear path with a defined endpoint.

By embracing these insights and applying the MOMENTuM process, you can create and sustain a culture that not only supports but propels your organization towards its strategic goals, ensuring long-term success and vitality.

IV

CALL TO ACTION

29

WHY NOW?

Why You Need to Address Your Culture NOW

One of the most insightful activities in writing this book was the interviews I conducted with business leaders. The interview protocol was pretty simple. I asked them about the best work culture they were ever a part of, and the worst, and what made each of them so. If you didn't just skip to this chapter, you have read a lot of their stories already, but there were many you didn't read too – I just couldn't include all of them. Not a surprise, but nearly all of them described aspects of their cultures - good and bad - that are related to the factors within the Momentum Framework. The quantitative research provided hard data that validated the inclusion of each factor, but the stories from the interviews provided color and brought life to them. The recurring themes from the interviews matched the issues that popped in the data – a clear validation of the model.

But while that coherence was welcome and added certainty that I had it right, that was not the most powerful insight from the interviews. The elements that really shook me were the clarity of the stories they told, and their assessment of the current state of culture in their organizations and the effect it was having on their employees.

Firstly, I was blown away by how clearly each interviewee could recall their best and worst cultures. EVERY interviewee shared their perspective on those work experiences in the form of stories and examples, and the level of detail in these anecdotes was astounding. Someone would share a story like it was yesterday, and many responded that it was actually over 30 years ago. When people would share their negative culture stories, I could almost instantly see the residual trauma on their face and in their voice. The memories were so vivid, and the old feelings were so palpable. Conversely, when they shared their positive stories about the best culture they ever were a part of, you would think they were telling you about when they rode their first roller coaster or the birth of their first child. Their faces would light up, and the air of nostalgia was just so real.

I share this to add weight to something you probably already know, but it bears repeating. We spend a tremendous part of our lives in our jobs. And our careers are sources of many of the biggest triumphs and emotional injuries that we have in our lives. We all know what it feels like to be in the wrong job, or with a company in decline, or to have a terrible manager - so I won't belabor those points. But, to a person, each interviewee had such an overwhelmingly positive reaction to their best culture. Many of them commented without solicitation – the ones that were not working for the best culture now – that they would drop what they were doing "in a heartbeat", if members of that team offered to "get the band back together". Their good culture experiences had such an impact on them that they would uproot their career to try to relive it. It shows you the positive impact it had on them - how fundamental it is to their career and psyche, and how it shaped their perceptions of leadership and connection for the rest of their lives.

Secondly, several of them are yearning for it again, because their current culture is so far removed from their best environment ever. So much so, that it stands in stark relief against what they know is possible. While it is hard to recreate past memories, it is not difficult to improve upon what many shared about their current cultures. The shift to remote or hybrid working environments has had a meaningful negative impact on the connection their coworkers have with each other and the organization at large. The interviewees that remarked that they were living their best culture were almost 100% in working environments like what they had pre-COVID.

The ones that were no longer living their best cultural experience thought the current culture was not only not a driver of their business, but actually a tangible liability. And they were empathetic enough to realize that as more experienced senior executives, the weaker culture wasn't affecting them nearly as much as their younger, front-line workers. They all shared that it was not uncommon for some of their newer hires to have never met a coworker, or that many people that had been with the company for over a year, had never met their manager in person.

In these kinds of situations, it is naïve to think that these people do not feel isolated. And expecting them to feel a meaningful connection to the company is just not reasonable, or at least not likely. And if so, expecting them to deliver their best work, or even just a solid effort, might be just as unreasonable. They likely view the company in a very transactional way and may be closer to that "mercenary" persona that I described earlier, than you might think.

For most companies, simply turning back the clock to 2019 just isn't possible. It may be completely impractical and even unproductive to return to your past working paradigms. But that shouldn't preclude you from understanding where your gaps in Connection and Capability are today and taking steps to bridge them. It will not be free, but nothing worth pursuing is ever free or even cheap.

But, depending upon your business model, it may not be relevant if you can afford to invest in bringing people together and building culture. You may need to assess whether your business can survive long-term if you don't. But conversely, the data shows that if you can create a Momentum Culture, the competitive advantage you can realize in the market will likely pay off tenfold.

But that is not why I am suggesting you address your culture now. We have already discussed the business value. I am talking about human value now. We all know what it feels like when you are in a culture that is creating and delivering Momentum to the business and everyone in it. I have shared the power in the stories I heard, but I am sure you have stories of your own that are just as powerful – you know the impact a great culture can have. So, as an organizational leader, the opportunity you have is breath-taking. So much so that I hope many of you view it as a responsibility and not an opportunity. Not by buying gourmet lunches or foosball tables, but by investing in your fundamentals – building the key capabilities and connection points you need to become a great company that wins consistently. You can give your employees the best experience of their lives, one that they will remember forever and that will shape their worldview on life and work. And if you pull it off, that will likely be your best culture ever too.

Get to work. Reach out if you think I can help you put a new, great band together.

Matt Prostko

30
ACKNOWLEDGEMENTS AND THE IMPORTANCE OF FUN

Momentum Cultures are Fun

I led an office for a consulting company that had a great culture, and I am sure it still does today. But every company goes through ebbs and flows, and at one point, there seemed to be some cracks forming in the plaster. Cheers to the CEO at the time for taking it seriously, being proactive, and trying to ascertain the issue and solve the problem, if there was one.

In a listening tour, people were commenting that they just weren't having as much fun at work anymore. That was a huge concern for the CEO, a leader that took great pride in the culture and knew that their brand of "fun" was something that customers really reacted positively to.

So, to quantify and get a better understanding of the issue, they instituted a weekly "Fun Survey" that asked two simple questions – "Did you have fun this week at work?", and then simply "Why or Why not?" The responses were carved up, and leaders were challenged to identify what was going on in their offices and improve it based on lessons learned.

Fortunately, my office was consistently scoring well, often a 5.0/5.0. So, naturally, the question was asked, "what is going on in that office, and how can we replicate it?" Well, if a simple "copy and paste" solution, was going to work, culture would not be the challenge that it is, and no one would bother to read any book about it, yet alone this one. But I explained the situation as best I could – that the group simply loved working together as a team, and the more they got to do that, the more fun they tended to have. The other offices did their best to improve –

they created "Fun Committees" to try to manufacture some fun. But let's face it, if you have a "Fun Committee", no one is having any fun.

So why was our team having fun? To be honest, some of it was blind luck. We were fortunate to land some really friendly, highly competent people that leaned into the team dynamic and created an amazing work environment. But there was some intentional recruiting that is worth noting. I believe that there are traits that are indexed to high-performance cultures, and you should consider recruiting for them, depending on your environment, business model, and strategy, of course.

- *Curiosity:* Curious people want to learn new things – both about their work, and just as importantly, about the people around them. Truly curious people can't stop learning or getting smarter. When they see broken patterns, they are compelled to resolve them, and in the process, they learn exponentially, and you don't need to pay for programs to accomplish that. They do it themselves at a faster rate than you could ever manage with a program. Moreover, that curiosity can often be perceived as empathy - demonstrating an authentic interest in your teammates. That empathy creates connections – real bonds with teammates that a fun committee cannot duplicate. In my interviews, I would actively create opportunities for candidates to demonstrate pure curiosity, and I wouldn't end the interview until I felt I had objectively assessed this trait.

- *Intelligence:* In athletics you will hear people say, "You can't coach speed". I liken that to intelligence in the workplace. You can't teach smart. I will take smarts over experience every day. Smart, curious people will figure it out, whatever it is. They will ask lots of questions (curious), and the right questions (smart), until they do. Also, I have always found that smart people are very often funny – they just pick up on insights a hair faster than others, and they tend to surprise people. So, I engaged an assessment expert to create an intelligence assessment that had been validated to not be culturally biased, and to simply identify strengths in core pattern-matching.

235

- *Positivity:* Some people just tend to believe that everything is going to work out positively, and they tend to see the interesting or light side of things. They can be serious, but not at the expense of the moment and the opportunity. In small group work like we engaged in, one person with a negative or cynical lean can siphon the energy from the team. But I often found that truly intelligent people tended to be positive – perhaps because they always saw possibility instead of hopelessness. Again, I actively probed candidates around challenges and setbacks, looking for optimism, but also with a high sensitivity to "faux positivity" that was forced or inauthentic.

- *Extroversion:* We were a consulting organization. So, by nature, the work is done by small teams, and often done in front of client groups. Introverts can do that job, but over time, it can tend to exhaust them. That does not mean that there is no place for introverts to in a Momentum Culture. But, by and large, cultures – high-performance or otherwise – are created by the chemistry of people interacting. I believe that extroverts love coming together and working (Connection), and when they get to mix with other smart, curious, and positive people (Capability), they are happy, they have fun, and they do their best work - so much so, that it doesn't feel like work (Momentum).

And that might be the best definition of a Momentum culture - fun and effortless. People doing the most challenging work of their lives, with people that challenge them back. Enjoying the process, forming relationships that go beyond the work, creating bonds that enrich life, that change the fight over hybrid work from "having to go to the office" to "getting to go to the office".

I can honestly say that I had little to do with that magic culture – as I said, it was the chemistry of a unique group of people that really liked working with each other. But immodestly, I did do a few things right. I intentionally and actively recruited for those traits. I found the smartest, most curious, positive extroverts I could find, put them together, and got the hell out of the way. I tried to enable them - not manage them. I tried to coach them hard, because they were "A" players that could handle that, but I clearly signaled that I approved of and supported the fun.

And even though I was the leader, I tried to make sure I was not the center of the action - they were the action. But they were wonderful, generous people who were always tugging at my sleeve and inviting me into the fun. Like everyone that I interviewed, I will never forget that and would work with any of them the minute they called.

To all of you – you know who you are - thanks for inspiring me to write this book, and as always, for your friendship and support.

Matt

REFERENCES

Boyd, J. (n.d.). OODA Loop. Retrieved from Wikipedia: https://en.wikipedia.org/wiki/OODA_loop

Businesswire. (2012). *BTS to Host Executive Panel Featuring Executives from The Coca-Cola Company, Kimberly-Clark and Walmart.* Retrieved from BusinessWire: https://www.businesswire.com/news/home/20120412005935/en/BTS-to-Host-Executive-Panel-Featuring-Executives-from-The-Coca-Cola-Company-Kimberly-Clark-and-Walmart

Conant, D. (2020, July 19). *Trust is Not a Soft Skill.* Retrieved from Conant Leadership: https://conantleadership.com/trust-is-not-a-soft-skill/

Covey, S. M. (2006). *The Speed of Trust.*

Covey, S. M. (2016). The Connection Between Employee Trust and Financial Performance. *Harvard Business Review.*

Daniels, W. (1997). *The Change-Able Organization.* Jossey-Bass.

Deloitte. (2016). Global Human Capital Trends. *Global Human Capital Trends.*

Ebbinghaus, H. (1885). *The Forgetting Curve.*

Groysberg, B. (2018). The Leader's Guide to Corporate Culture. *Harvard Business Review.*

Hammond, J. (1998). The Hidden Traps in Decision Making. *Harvard Business Review.*

Hewlett Packard. (n.d.). *The 9 Day Fortnight.* Retrieved from Hewlett Packard Company Archives: https://www.hewlettpackardhistory.com/item/the-nine-day-fortnight/

Kotter, J. (2008). *Sense of Urgency.*

Kotter, J. (2011). *Corporate Culture and Performance.*

Mankins, M. (2005). Turning Great Strategy into Great Performance. *Harvard Business Review.*

Microsoft. (2021). *A study of 61,000 Microsoft employees suggests remote work is bad for communication between different teams.* Retrieved from Business Insider: https://www.businessinsider.com/remote-work-working-from-home-study-microsoft-meetings-2021-9

Project Management Institute. (2014). *The High Cost of Low Performance.*

Rawson, A. (2013). The Truth About Customer Experience. *Harvard Business Review.*

Russell, M. (2024). *How to Build—and Improve—Company Culture.* Harvard University.

Sorenson, J. B. (2001). *The Strength of Corporate Culture and the Reliability of Firm Performance.* Cambridge, MA.

Statista. (2024, January 10). *Workplace learning and development - statistics & facts.* Retrieved from Statista: https://www.statista.com/topics/4281/workplace-learning-and-development/#statisticChapter

Willis Towers Watson. (2012). The Global Workforce Study.

Wiseman, L. (2010). *Multipliers: How the Best Leaders Make Everyone Smarter,".*

Yang, L. (2021). The effects of remote work on collaboration among information workers. Nature, 43-54.

Zak, P. (2017). *The Neuroscience in Building High Performance Trust Cultures.* Retrieved from CLO: https://www.chieflearningofficer. com/2017/02/09/neuroscience-building-trust-cultures/#:~:text=Un- surprisingly%2C%20those%20who%20work%20in,Create%20a%20 High%20Trust%20Culture?

Zippia. (n.d.). *Social Isolation in Remote Work.* Retrieved from eddy: https://eddy.com/hr-encyclopedia/social-isolation-in-remote-work/

www.ingramcontent.com/pod-product-compliance
Lightning Source LLC
Chambersburg PA
CBHW061156240326
R18026500001B/R180265PG41519CBX00010B/13